MOM'S EVERYTHING BOOK
FOR SONS

Other Books in This Series

MOM'S EVERYTHING BOOK FOR SONS

• practical ideas for a quality relationship •

BECKY FREEMAN

WOMEN OF FAITH™

ZONDERVAN™

GRAND RAPIDS, MICHIGAN 49530 USA

ZONDERVAN™

Mom's Everything Book for Sons
Copyright © 2003 by Becky Freeman and Women of Faith, Inc.

Requests for information should be addressed to:

Zondervan, *Grand Rapids, Michigan 49530*

Library of Congress Cataloging-in-Publication Data

Freeman, Becky, 1959–
   Mom's everything book for sons : practical ideas for a quality relationship / by Becky Freeman.
     p. cm.
Includes bibliographical references.
   ISBN 0-310-24295-9
   1. Preteens. 2. Mothers and sons. 3. Sons—Psychology. 4. Parenting—Religious aspects. 5. Mothers—Life skills guides. I. Title.
   HQ777.15.F74 2003
   306.874'3–dc21   2002156630

Published in association with the literary agency of Alive Communications, Inc., 7680 Goddard Street, Suite 200, Colorado Springs, CO 80920.

Interior design by Susan Ambs

Printed in the United States of America

03 04 05 06 /❖ DC/ 10 9 8 7 6 5 4 3 2 1

To my dear friends,
Melissa and Joshua Gantt,
Earth Mother and Teen Angel
In memory of love that never dies
That of the love between mother and son
Joshua Gantt
1982–2002

Contents

How to Read This Book

Knowing how busy and hectic a typical mom's life can be, I've purposely designed this book to be mom and kid friendly. Each chapter starts with a story, usually filled with plenty of humor. (My belief is that a good dose of laughter always helps the medicine of application go down a little easier.) You can read these chapters in chronological order or enjoy this book like handfuls of popcorn, tasting the sections that most interest you. Ideas for connecting with your son and Just for Fun activities are scattered throughout and can be applied at will.

First, a special word about the Bible study portions of this book: In *Leap over a Wall*, an insightful book about the life of King David, Eugene Peterson opens his chapter about the prophet Samuel coming to anoint the boy David as future king by writing, "Samuel was an old man with his beard down to his knees. I learned this from my mother, from whom I first heard the story." Peterson's mother told biblical stories in such vivid color that she literally brought the characters and settings to life for him when he was young. Later in the chapter, Peterson confesses,

> Throughout my childhood, in my mother's telling of the story, I became David. I was always David. I'm

still David. It's the intent and skill of this scriptural storyteller to turn everyone who reads or hears the story into realizing something essentially davidic about him—or herself: "In my insignificant, sheep-keeping obscurity, I am chosen."

After reading these lines and rereading the rich account of King David's life, I decided to write all of the devotional moments in this book around the subject of David. In my book for mothers of daughters *(Mom's Everything Book for Daughters)*, each devotional was about various subjects, various biblical characters. Girls seem to enjoy a variety of topics, the same way our feminine brains love browsing magazines or gift stores.

But our sons, ah, our sons are waffles. And active waffles at that. To keep their attention, we are going to grab those beautiful, boyish minds with a continuing story that starts with an ordinary young guy, who, through failure and triumph, becomes a man after God's own heart. What better way to bond with your son than to pique his interest in one of the greatest biblical sagas of all time?

Therefore, throughout this book, I will be closing each chapter with scriptures, stories, and activities that center around the amazing life of David. Moms, I will give you the raw materials to draw upon, but like Eugene Peterson's mother, you will have to be the one to infuse these devotional moments with energy, enthusiasm, and life! With your personal excitement mixed in with an exciting biblical story line, your boy may grow up to slay all sorts of evil giants with the smooth stones of faith you pass on to him.

Throughout this book, at the close of the Bible study time, I'll suggest a Scripture for your son to write down and keep handy or to memorize.

Here's a fun rhyme to share with your son before bedtime to encourage him to hide the Word of God in his heart:

> *Keep a verse in your pocket*
> *Or a Scripture in your head*
> *And you'll never be alone*
> *At night when you're in bed.*

Read on.

Chapter 1

Midnight Taco Runs

Bonding with Your Son

I met one of my dearest friends, Gracie Malone, just in time for the arrival of puberty—that is, the puberty of my eldest son, Zach, followed quickly by his brother Zeke, and then my daughter, Rachel. Many adolescent episodes later, Gracie is still the best shoulder to lean on as I finish mothering my fifteen-year-old son, Gabe, the caboose of our family train.

The first time I met Gracie, I was in the throes of agony over Zach's ugly thirteen-year-old hairstyle of choice. It was the '80s and the year of the Bangs That Hang Over the Eyes and Into the Cereal Bowl. How I longed to see the actual face of my offspring, to view once more his handsome brown eyes. But, alas, for months he remained hidden behind a thick curtain of hair.

As a mother who had raised three sons into manhood and withstood the tide of teenage turmoils, Gracie offered the sort of advice I craved.

"Gracie, how will I survive raising three boys?" I asked her one day as I sank into her overstuffed living room chair and nestled her small dachshund, Porsche, close to my side.

She smiled, leaned back on a couch pillow, and said, "Hairstyles will come and go. You'll look back and laugh at the small things that irritated you so much at the time. Let the small stuff go if you can. The most important thing I can tell you, Becky, about raising boys is to never neglect midnight taco runs."

"What?"

Gracie grinned and replied, "Look for opportunities to bond with your boys whenever you can, Beck. When my youngest son, Jason, was a teen, he would often look at me mischievously late on a weekend night and ask, 'Are you hungry for tacos?' With those words, I'd grab my car keys and we'd head to Jack in the Box for a fast-food fix. We had some of our best conversations during those late-night jaunts."

"Why did Jason prefer to go on these mom and son dates after dark?" I queried. Even Porche cocked her doggie head curiously to one side.

"Why do you think?"

"So no one would see him cruising the streets with his mother in broad daylight."

"You got it, babe. No telling what being seen in public, riding in the car with your mom, could do to a boy's cool reputation."

And thus I was initiated into being a mother of teens—a state I've been living in for the past decade, with three years left in my term as mom-of-a-kid-at-home.

Of late, I've been hit with the realization that my time with my lastborn is short, and am curtailing several career activities so I can spend more time with Gabe before he graduates into the world of grown-ups. My friend Liz Curtis Higgs once shared that her daughter thought she worked at the local airport because she flew out of town to speak so often. My schedule, I thought, was pretty light compared to most authors and speakers. However, I was stopped short by an incident that occurred a few months ago.

I pulled into the driveway of our lakeside home, returning from speaking at a weekend retreat. I wearily walked into the kitchen and hugged Gabe in greeting.

"Where have you been?" he asked.

"I've been in Georgia for two days," I answered.

He shrugged in slight surprise before answering, "Oh. I thought you were at Wal-Mart."

Now I admit I can spend a good long afternoon wandering down the endless aisles of our local Super Wal-Mart, but this was ridiculous. Was my presence at home that invisible?

After the shock of Gabe's comment wore off a bit, I went on a mission to find out what this kid really thought about me—as mom material, that is. So I poured two stiff glasses of Dr Pepper (the state soft drink of Texas) and invited him to join me at the kitchen bar.

Leaning over the counter, I begin my interrogation. "Gabe, I need to know that I've made some sort of impression on you as your mother. It's frightening to think you've barely noticed my absence for two whole days and nights!

Tell me, son, what will you remember most when you think about me as your mom?"

He took a thoughtful sip of his soda before answering. "Well, Mom, I'll remember looking at the back of a car through the windshield, telling you what kind of burger or taco I want to order, and laughing a lot."

I breathed an enormous sigh of relief. Thank you, Lord! I haven't totally failed as a mother! I might not have served many home-cooked meals, but at least I had followed Gracie's advice. I took advantage of countless taco runs—in daylight and moonlight. Not only that, but my child cherished the laughter that so often bounced around the walls of our minivan. If Gabe remembers me as The Mom Who Laughed, my maternal life would not have been lived in vain. A sense of humor is a terrific quality in a parent, is it not? Okay, I know it would probably be better if my son remembered me praying on my knees at 5:00 A.M., or reading the family Bible at bedtime. But being merry most of the time should count for at least a few mothering brownie points, I should think.

All in all, I was pleased with Gabe's basic thoughts about life with his mother, though I hope by graduation day he can add a few more good memories of Mom to his current short list of fast food and funniness.

Thankfully, I still have three years left to figure out how to cook a nice pot roast dinner, become a spiritual giant, and pare down my shopping time at Wal-Mart.

Ten Ways to Enjoy Your Boy

Today I heard radio host and author Dennis Prager talk of how few parents really enjoy their kids and what a shame that is! Parenting is hard work, but it can also be a

SHOOTIN' THE BREEZE

Try asking your son what good things he will remember most about you as his mother. Then share with him a couple of good memories you will always cherish of him.

great deal of fun. Here are some ideas to spark your imagination with interesting and fun activities that can help bond you with your son.

1. Read a chapter book, one chapter each night. Pick a book with a lot of fast-moving action, something that will hold a kid's full attention. (See book recommendations later in this chapter.)
2. Shoot hoops. Even if you aren't a natural athlete, boys crave the attention of admiring moms and love showing off their skills. Badminton and croquet also provide great backyard fun for moms and sons.
3. Buy a plastic model airplane or car or other object at a hobby store and work on it together as a continuing project.
4. Teach your son to play a new card game, dominoes, or a board game. This can include his friends. They will think you are the coolest mom in the neighborhood.
5. Learn to rollerblade or bike with your son—if you dare!
6. Go on a Mom and Me Date—no other siblings allowed. Let your son pick a parent-approved movie and where to eat.
7. Go fishing. Even if you can't stand to put the worm on the hook or take the fish off the hook, your son will probably enjoy doing this task for you. (It makes him feel manly!)

8. On a pretty day, go somewhere scenic. Take art supplies—paints, sketchbook, charcoal pencils, and maybe even easels—and both of you try drawing or painting the scene in front of you.

9. Pitch a tent in the backyard and let a couple of his buddies come over for a sleep-out. Cook wieners and marshmallows over a grill or in the fireplace on long sticks or metal clothes hangers bent straight.

10. Learn to play a harmonica together. There's a Klutz book complete with harmonica and instructions. Check www.klutz.com.

JUST FOR FUN!

If you want to laugh with your son, this activity is a surefire winner in a crowd of bored boys. Take a drinking straw and put one end in your mouth, the other end in the small of your armpit. Blow until you hear astounding and obnoxious sounds emerging from your arm. This is guaranteed to delight the male species and leave them begging for straws to try it themselves. Best not performed in a public place.

Best Books for Boys

Reading aloud to children has to be one of the best all-around mother-child bonding activities of all time. My sister recently purchased an enormous chaise lounge big enough for herself, her eight-year-old son, and her two-year-old daughter to snuggle up together for nightly read-aloud sessions.

When my boys were young they loved when I read them *The Wind in the Willows*, The Boxcar Children series, The Chronicles of Narnia, *A Wrinkle in Time*, *Little House in the Big Woods*, Pippi Longstocking books, and— though some of his writing borders on the bizarre—anything by wacky British writer Roald Dahl, from *Charlie and the Chocolate Factory* to *James and the Giant Peach* to *The BFG*. I began reading short chapter books interspersed with illustrated books to my boys when they were very young. Our weekly trip to the library, which was within walking distance from our home, was the highlight of our week, and I was just as eager as they were to get home and read our latest finds.

After reading the lovely and moving book *Beauty* about a boy's love for his horse, my son Zeke read every book written by Bill Wallace and even enjoyed a friendly correspondence with this principal-turned-award-winning children's author from Oklahoma. Most authors love hearing from kids and will answer them if at all possible and many have websites. I have had some wonderful email conversations with kids who enjoyed my Camp Wanna Banana Mystery Series (Waterbrook), including one from an enthusiastic eleven-year-old aspiring author. She writes, "I hate to bother you with all these questions, but I plan to be a writer for my whole life." Isn't that great?

POINTS TO PONDER

According to Judy Ford, author of *Wonderful Ways to Love a Child*, "Enjoying spontaneous, uninhibited play is a natural and refreshing expression of your vitality. When you allow your adult worries and responsibilities to subside for a while, a miracle of togetherness happens and lasting memories are made. Playing with your children does not have to be expensive nor a day-long affair. No fancy toys are needed, nor elaborate plans. Deborah taught her kids to juggle using marshmallows; Tony looks forward to summer months when he can play scotch, an updated version of hide-n-seek, with his kids and the neighbors. A lighthearted pillow fight while you change the beds, or a quick game of tag in the backyard—spontaneous, fun for everyone, and good exercise too!"[1]

---

[1]Judy Ford, *Wonderful Ways to Love a Child* (Berkeley: Conari Press, 1995), 72.

A Boy After God's Own Heart

Read 1 Samuel 16:1–13

Saul was a good king gone bad, and this hurt the heart of God. So he sent Samuel, his prophet, to find God's chosen man who would take Saul's place on the throne and anoint him with oil. (The oil symbolized holiness and was used to set people apart for God's service. Each king and high priest of Israel was anointed with oil.)

1. Who of Jesse's sons did Samuel think God was going to choose? Why? (vv. 6, 7)
2. What does the Lord look at when he looks at people? What do human beings look for? (v. 7)
3. So many times God chooses the most unlikely people to do the most amazing things! David was just a shepherd boy; the great warrior Gideon was a coward; the leader Moses was afraid to speak in front of people. Why do you think God chooses the weakest people to do the greatest things?

Just Do It!

Your son may sometimes feel he is just a plain ol' kid in the family. Assure him that God has great things in mind for him. Tell your son what some of his best inner qualities are and have him write them down on a card to keep in his Bible as a bookmark reminder of what God sees in him.

A Verse in Your Pocket

On the back of your son's bookmark card, have him write this verse and try to memorize it:

Man looks at the outward appearance, but the Lord looks at the heart.

1 SAMUEL 16:7

Chapter 2

"Hey Mom! Watch This!"

Your Son's Need for Female Praise

I was in the emergency room with a head-to-toe outbreak of poison ivy, waiting for a doctor to help relieve my agony. As I was waiting, I heard the terrified screams of a young boy in the examining room next door. "Pleeease Mister Doctor, don't do that! Don't hurt me! No! No! Please, please, please. . ."

Between the heart-rending pleas, screams, and sobs, I heard enough grown-up conversation to surmise that the boy, named Robert, had fallen on a seashell, which cut his knee deeply. He was in the painful process of getting the wound cleaned, followed by shots for deadening the pain. By the time the ordeal of the first stage was over, the boy, the father, the grandmother, the doctor, the nurse, and all the patients within hearing distance were emotionally spent. I wiped my own tears, remembering the terror of being on the receiving end of a suturing needle when I was a small child. Suddenly, I knew what I had to do.

I rounded the corner, peeked in the curtain, and asked if I could talk to the little guy for a minute. I quietly explained to the doctor that I wrote children's books, had been a first-grade teacher, and then assured him I spoke fluent kid-talk. He shrugged his weary shoulders and reluctantly nodded. "You're welcome to give it a try."

The little fellow looked at me, tears streaming and chest heaving. His knee looked as though a small shark had taken a bite out of it. I tried not to wince and instead looked at the boy's enormous eyes, smiled my biggest nice-teacher smile, and said, "Hey there, Robert, I couldn't help overhearing all the excitement from next door! What happened to you? And, wow, aren't you a *big brave boy!*" (I decided the best route would be to act "as if.")

What followed was nothing short of a miracle. The boy stopped mid-scream, sniffed a few times, held up his skinny little arm, flexing a muscle the size of a walnut, and with manly pride exclaimed, "Yeah, and I'm *strong* too!" The doctor blinked in surprise, then asked if I could possibly stay for the remainder of the operation. Robert and I passed the time swapping stories, and in a few minutes, he was in complete stitches (the laughing kind and the sewing kind). Robert's father, on his knees beside his son with tears in his eyes, looked up at me and asked, "Are you an angel?"

Though I could not answer in the affirmative, I do believe I flew home on the wings of the indescribably terrific feeling of having helped ease a small, frightened boy's pain by ignoring what was, and holding up a mirror to what I believed he could be—a brave, big-muscled, and very manly six-year-old.

A Boy's Gnawing Need for Female Adulation

Bill and Anabel Gilham are two of my favorite people. In their seventies now, they are relaxing into the golden years of marriage and enjoying each other to the hilt, but they spent the first twenty years of marriage in torturous turmoil. Bill was a man with a fragile ego, desperately needing to prove himself as a macho male. Anabel was a pleaser and a perfectionist. The combination proved nearly fatal to their marriage, until God broke down the walls of dysfunction and opened their hearts and minds to understanding deep truths about males and females.

One of the most profound things Anabel discovered in her search to understand her husband is that a man's needs are not all that complex, but they are very deep. And one of the biggest needs of a man is to receive sincere praise (not surface flattery) from a woman, and this need begins in the earliest days of childhood. Who is the first female boys look to for reassurance of their manly worth? None other than Mom. I wonder how often we mothers realize we're holding our sons' fragile male egos in the palms of our hands.

In the Gilhams' book, *He Said, She Said,* Bill writes,

> From the very onset of male-female relations, female praise is an unequalled balm to males.... It's not that we have an ego problem although admittedly, some guys overdo it. God created all males with a specific need for female praise. We were born with it just as females were born with a need for male TLC.

Along with the book, the Gilhams give live conferences about the core needs of men and women. Bill illustrates this innate desire for female praise with an example of a six-year-old kid who is hanging by his heels from a limb of the apple tree in his backyard. "Who does he yell at to come out and see him? Mom! 'Hey, Mom! C'mere!'" In his folksy Oklahoma accent, Bill tells audiences that

> this little guy is trying to demonstrate to the main female in his life what a "hoss" he is and that he can do a physical, masculine thing she can't do. He wants her to be astounded at his daring! If she steps to the door and says, "Wow! How can you stay up there like that? Aren't you afraid you'll fall?" it thrills him to death. Guys love that sort of thing. It makes us feel male. We come factory-equipped that way.

Anabel, in her sweet southern way, interrupts Bill for a moment and asks women, "Can you imagine what would happen if I were that little boy's mom, and I decided to go out and demonstrate my expertise as a tree-hanger and out-perform him?" It's important that mothers understand that this is the time our sons need applause and praise from the sidelines, not competition in their spotlight. Our boys are testing their masculine wings.

This may fly in the face of feminist philosophy, but my guess is that what Bill says in the following summary will ring true with every mother who watches her son leave her shadow to prove himself a man in the world.

"Let's look in on the same boy at age ten or so," Bill continues,

> He's weaning himself off Mom, and developing an interest in ten-year-old girls. He can't hang in the tree and holler, "Hey girls, look!" That would be uncool. So instead, when he sees the girls approach-

ing, he gives them his best tree-hanging routine complete with sound effects to attract their attention. Then he imagines that they are thinking the same thoughts Mom used to express. "Wow, look at that!" He gets that same good feeling, and it reassures him that they think he's a hunk.

Once he's in high school, the whole process gets more sophisticated, so tree-hanging is out. High school women expect something more spectacular, so our young man becomes an athlete. He sweats blood on the football field, and when he finally gets his letterman's jacket, he practices looking, walking and acting cool in front of the mirror. Once he gets all this down pat, he strolls down the halls of the high school in his jacket and basks in the admiring glances of the girls. . . . It's the way God made us.

And just to bring the point home, Bill concludes, "Hey, when the camera zooms in on the guy who scored in an NFL game, what does he say? 'Hi, Mom!' I know he's putting us on, but he doesn't say, 'Hi, Dad,' does he? It bears repeating—we males need female praise, especially from the female we love."

Since you and I, the mothers of sons, are the very first females our boys fall in love with, let's not disappoint them. Be ready to give them buckets full of affirmation to help build their self-image of manhood, as they enter a world that isn't always as encouraging as we wish it were.

"Cheering can consist of simply waving the pom-poms and jumping up and down a few times or simply saying 'Yay!' Or if you're really happy about something they did, why not try writing a cheer, harking back to your high school days? Perhaps the garbage cheer of 'Pack it up, take it out, gooooo Jason!' You might just cheer yourself up along the way."[2]

> ### POINTS TO PONDER
>
> Charlene Bombich in *365 Ways to Connect with Your Kids* has a good idea when it comes to helping build our sons' egos. She writes, "Get yourself some pom-poms. They're cheap and can be found in most toy stores. Keep them handy and occasionally pull them out to cheer when your child does something notable—or even when he or she comes in the door after school. Or when he takes out the garbage. She helps set the table. They don't argue for more than an hour. They get home on time. He plays with his baby brother. He smiles at you, just when you needed a smile most. She gets a good grade. He gets an okay grade but it's better than the one before that. You get the idea: it's something right you've noticed.

Ten Ways to Make Your Boy Feel Like a Man

1. Ask, "Will you come help me? I need a guy with muscles to help me carry in these groceries!"(This still brings fifteen-year-old Gabe to his feet, and he always carries as many sacks as he possibly can in one trip—to my openmouthed admiration, of course.)
2. Ask, "Did you know you look a lot like _____?" Fill in the blank with an admired movie star, musi-

---

[2]Charlene Bombich, *365 Ways to Connect with Your Kids* (Franklin Lakes, NJ: Career, 2001), 41.

cian, or athlete. Gabe is dark and handsome so he loves being compared to Elvis or Tom Cruise. My son-in-law, Jody, is our resident Brad Pitt.

3. Observe, then ask, "How do you think you got so smart at _____?" Fill in a school subject where you feel he is naturally gifted.

4. Catch him being good and then say, "I couldn't help noticing how great you were on the phone (or to the neighbor or new kid). It makes me feel so proud of your social skills."

5. Leave a surprise note on his bed or door thanking him for a task well done, even a small one (taking out trash, tending a sibling, cleaning his room, etc.).

6. Affirm him by saying, "God gave you so many talents, didn't he? What are some of the things you believe you do best?"

7. Watch for good behavior after he loses a game (this may take a few games!) and reward it by saying, "I was so proud of your sportsmanship on the field today, even though your team lost. You gave it your personal best and were gracious to the winners. Now that's what real men are made of!"

8. Win his heart by saying, "If I got to pick out any kid in the world to be my kid, I'd pick you in a heartbeat."

9. Every so often, out of the blue, gaze at him, rub his back, or tousle his hair and say, "I'm so lucky to be your mom."

10. Encourage his spiritual growth by commenting, "When you are kind, it warms my heart, and I see a peek of Jesus inside of you and the sort of wonderful man you are growing up to be."

Rent the movie *The Sound of Music* or *Swiss Family Robinson* and watch it with your son. Both films show obvious examples of the need for feminine praise and the results in terms of making a guy feel like a man. One of my favorite scenes is when the father in *Swiss Family Robinson* has just completed a tree house for his wife and is showing it to her for the very first time. This grown man is reduced to an anxious little boy, unable to breathe a sigh of relief until his wife offers the praise he is craving. Serve popcorn and soft drinks and, after the movie is over, enjoy a relaxed talk with your son about the need for female praise and the importance of finding a wife someday who will be his best cheerleader and encourager.

Other Encouragers

Because women are usually the most natural encouragers in a home, you may also be the best one to be on the lookout for other encouragers for your son—female or male! If you are married to a man who encourages, teaches, and provides a great example for your son, you have a treasure in your home. Applaud your husband often with verbal praise and notes of encouragement for being a great dad. However, in addition to you and your husband, keep an eye open for other mentors who will encourage and praise your son.

Our son Zeke has a keen interest in outdoor recreation. His dad was able to connect him with an enterprising young man named Brian Trusty, who owned and operated an adventure tour company called Sierra Quest.

For three summers, Zeke apprenticed under Brian, leading kids in rock climbing, white-water rafting, and hiking all over the country. Our church youth director also took an interest in Zeke and allowed him to start a coffee shop outreach on Saturday nights in our town. Zeke and his team hosted local bands, drama, game nights, even '60s beatnik-style poetry nights (complete with berets and bongo drums). Creativity reigned, the fun of it all ushered high school kids into a safe place where true friendships were formed, and Christ's gospel was shared. Zeke called it Soul Café and it was a great success.

Zeke also went with a team on a mission trip to Guatemala and enjoyed it so much. The next year he was asked to be a team leader. In addition, there were a couple of special high school coaches who encouraged Zeke's athletic ability, along with his Christian faith. Because of these and other mentors, Zeke had several outstanding letters of recommendation and an impressive resume before he ever graduated from high school. This kid had a blast growing up and was filled with confidence. Today he is an enthusiastic newlywed getting his degree in architecture, while his talented wife, Amy, is attending art school. In a heartbeat, Zeke would readily confess that it was the great role models (including, but also beyond, his family and extended family) who helped him become a happy, confident person—the sort of guy who walks into a room excited to meet new people or accept new challenges.

JUST FOR FUN

Ask your son to tell you one thing he really wants to learn to do. Perhaps it is something he already does, but he wants to become an expert at it. Try to find a man or woman who might mentor your son, even if it is just for an afternoon. For example, let's say your son says he has always wanted to learn how to fly-fish. Begin by thinking of any good family friends you know who love to fish and might be willing to take your son, and perhaps a buddy of his, out on a river for an afternoon. Call one of them and simply say, "My son would love to learn how to fish, but he needs someone to show him the ropes. I thought of you, remembering what a great fisherman you are, and wondered if there might be an afternoon in the coming month or two that you'd be willing to take him along and teach him the basics." Most men (or women or even older teens) will be enormously flattered that you asked, and enjoy the good feeling that comes from sharing their experience with a young person.

If you can't find someone and if you can afford it, check the Internet, yellow pages, or newspaper for lessons, special camps, or support groups centered around special hobbies. One summer my mother-in-law taught several grandchildren to swim. Another summer she gave them watercolor painting lessons. My father taught his grandsons to fish and golf. A grandmotherly neighbor, Mary Sue, taught my children how to make pottery and other art pieces in her craft room built especially for creativity. I remember back in my junior high days, my youth director giving several teens guitar lessons every Saturday afternoon. The ideas—and willing resources—are endless, and the results are exciting.

SHOOTIN' THE BREEZE

Ask your son to name three women he enjoys being around the most, and ask him to tell you why he feels that way. Then, if he's not too shy, ask him what sort of woman he thinks he'd like to marry someday.

A Boy After God's Own Heart

Read 1 Samuel 17

1. David's older brother Eliab made fun of David when he said he was willing to fight the giant Goliath with God's strength. Have you ever had someone make fun of you when you tried something new? How did it make you feel?

2. But God had been David's teacher and helper and encourager (in other words, his "mentor") throughout the time he was out in the field tending sheep. Verses 34–37 describe some ways that God helped build up David's confidence for this very moment in history. What were they?

3. Did David put his trust in the stones he slung, or in God? (v. 45)

Just Do It!

Find five smooth stones. Get a bright-colored paint pen and write one word on each stone: The / Lord / is / my / strength. Keep the stones somewhere special and, before you have to do something new, something that is a little bit scary and takes courage, hold these stones. Remember your strength comes from the same place David's came from: your teacher, your mentor, your God Almighty!

A Verse in Your Pocket

When Goliath taunted and teased David, the little shepherd boy had a great response. Memorize his words and know that David's God can also help you in times of trouble.

You come against me with sword and spear and javelin, but I come against you in the name of the Lord Almighty.

1 SAMUEL 17:45

Chapter 3

"I Gotta Be Me!"

*Fostering Your Son's Creativity
without Losing Your Mind*

Three years ago, when my eldest son, Zachary, was nineteen and would pop home for a visit from college, his father and I would take turns hyperventilating as we passed each other in the hallway, then comforting one another with the words "This too shall pass." At that time our son had a nifty, off-putting collection of piercings on his eyebrow and chin, and what he then believed to be the wisdom of the ages between his ears. This was followed by a small tattoo of a shark on his foot, which we thought outrageous, until he came home with an enormous oak tree tattooed across his back. He called it "the tree of life."

"Zach," I countered, "do you realize that when you are sixty or seventy years old, that giant oak of a tree will sag upon your wrinkled skin. It's going to look like a weeping willow by the time you are a grandfather."

I inwardly comfort myself that Zach will not be alone in his plight. Fifty or sixty years from now, nursing homes will be filled with elderly people trying to explain the original meaning of their collectively shriveling tattoos. "Nurse, I know this looks like an imprint of a raisin on my ankle, but when I was a youngster it was a rose, in full bloom, on my thigh."

Zach loved nothing more at this stage of his young life than to spend a long evening in pontification. His father and I would listen, sometimes for hours, as he defined in exhaustive detail the problems of humankind, the evil in the world, his determination to overcome it all with peace, love, and goodness—plus his special deep, inner knowledge. (Wasn't it Goethe who said, "Everyone believes in his youth that the world really began with him"?)

I would nod softly and think, *My son the prophet.*

"But people act afraid of me!" he'd say outraged, raising his hands and his voice in defiance. "Man, they judge me solely on the way I look!"

I would try hard not to comment: "Look, son, if I randomly poked holes in my head and stuck curtain rings through them, I suppose I too might get certain odd reactions from others." Instead, after one of his typical rantings, I simply said, "That's why God made mothers."

"What?" he asked, momentarily distracted from the subject of our downwardly spiraling universe.

"It's impossible for someone who diapered your bottom to be afraid of you, no matter how old you get to be or how much hardware you loop through your skin."

At this, his scowl melted into a boyish grin. The little peanut-butter kid I once hugged and kissed goodnight was still inside my nineteen-year-old puzzle of a young man. The atmosphere around us relaxed at once, like a balloon released of its contents. "Mom, that's what I love about you."

"What's that?"

"You are so simpleminded and sweet that even I can't intimidate you."

I decided to take this as a compliment, kissed his one unpierced brow, and offered to fix him a sandwich. My guru-son followed me to the kitchen, temporarily dropping the weight of the world, and picked up a lighter load. Eyeing the peanut butter, he asked felicitously, "Why do they say choosy mothers choose Jif? I mean, what are they trying to imply?"

I rolled my eyes with all the Shakespearean flair I could muster and, with a peanut-butter-dipped-dagger, responded, "To jelly, or not to jelly. *That* is the question."

The guru smiled a weary, grateful smile and simply said, "To jelly."

He didn't realize it at that moment, but it isn't prophets or poets or philosophers or pilgrims who hold the secrets to the universe. It's God, working through courageous mothers—armed with plenty of peanut butter and prayer—who see through the masks of struggling manhood, to a little boy hiding just below the surface of his skin (be it bearded, pierced, or tattooed).

For nervous mothers of teenage (or about-to-be teenage) boys, a note of encouragement: Within three months, the rings came out, replaced by an Abe Lincoln beard and a cowboy hat. In the past three years Zach has kept us on our toes and on our knees, as all "challenge children" are prone to do.

(Most families seem to be gifted with at least one child of this ilk.) However, tonight my now twenty-two-year-old son is enjoying a relaxing home video with me after having put in a hard day's work at his thriving lawn business. Earlier this summer's eve, he road on his sable horse, Cinnamon, near the ranch house where he now lives. He's planning on entering the armed services this coming fall to serve the country he once thought of with detachment and distrust. The events of September 11 brought many a disillusioned young person to his feet, right hand proudly placed over his heart, ready to defend an America that is flawed, for sure, but still the priceless home of the free and the brave.

So take heart, moms, with the boys under your roof who give you premature gray hairs. Some of them just take a little longer to grow up than others. Be patient, and don't take their fads and phases too seriously. Most of their experiments are harmless and short-lived. And the ones that aren't often teach our sons hard lessons they needed to learn, and perhaps couldn't learn any other way. Some prodigal sons have to return for several worldly pig-slop "tastings" before the truth permanently dawns: "Yes, this really is pig-slop. I believe I'll go home for roast beef now." There are many trials and errors on the road to becoming good, wise men. A mother's prayers are powerful forces in helping sons through this pilgrimage. So is our patience and tolerance. As Logan Pearsall Smith wisely observed, "Don't laugh at a youth for his affections; he's only trying on one face after another till he finds his own."

And find it, in time, he will.

Nurturing Their Creative Spirit

In the spirit of being less sensible, what do you do about your son who wants to experiment with a crazy fad?

POINTS TO PONDER

I'll never forget the afternoon I went to pick up my oldest boys, Zeke and Zach, from a visit with a friend. They must have been about six and seven years old.

"Mom," Zach complained as soon as he plopped himself in the front seat of the car, "it was raining outside. There were great mud puddles everywhere, and Jason's mother wouldn't even let us play in them." Big pause, big sigh, and then he added, "I'm so glad you aren't sensible like all the other kids' moms."

Is there an area of mothering where you can be a little less sensible and a lot more fun?

I have two rules for dealing with "iffy" fashion statements:

1. I won't embarrass you if you don't embarrass me.
2. If it is temporary, and can be undone, I am much more likely to say yes to their creativity.

Here's a prime example. When Gabe was about eleven, he begged for me to let him dye his hair blue. Hmmm. I had to admit, this would be a temporary change, his brown hair would grow back in time. Would it embarrass me to be walking alongside a blue-headed kid? Well, perhaps a little. Especially in my hometown. I also had a hunch it was against school policy.

Compromise? We went on vacation to Florida during the summer, and it was there that I granted my son's wish and let him dye his hair bleach white, then a brilliant blue. He looked . . . interesting, to say the least. However, because no one knew us in Destin and his dark locks would grow back before school started, it was no big deal.

My sons' choices of clothing have sometimes given my heart cause to skip a beat. Thankfully, Gabe entered high school about the time that the preppy look was back in style, so his wardrobe choices have been no problem. Zach and Zeke, however, entered hallowed high school halls during the age of grunge. I'll never forget the day I walked into the school office to sign Zeke out for a trip to the dentist. He casually walked in the door and all I could do was blink and then stare. It was near the holidays, and Zeke had dressed himself, shall we say, festively for the occasion. He wore a red felt Santa hat, a white T-shirt with striped suspenders holding up a pair of baggy khaki shorts. His skinny legs were covered with a pair of red thermal underwear and he had chosen a pair of cowboy boots to complete the ensemble.

At just that moment, the principal strolled by, looked at Zeke, then back at me, shook his head, and said, "Mrs. Freeman, he's your son." I looked up at the principal helplessly and said, "And he's your student," but what we were both really thinking is that Zeke Freeman was his *own* person. Unique in every way.

For the most part, I let Zach and Zeke be the individuals they wanted to be. Their favorite place to shop was Goodwill, and the best "finds" were old employee shirts with names on them, like "Jerry" emblazoned above the pocket of a Pizza Palace uniform. They enjoyed their unique status, provided harmless entertainment for students and teachers alike, and gave me more than a few laughs.

Yesterday I heard a poignant story by Dr. Phil (Oprah's right-hand therapist). He told the story of a father who constantly rode his teenage son about the length of his hair and the baggy, grungy clothes he wore. Then one day, the boy was playing basketball and suddenly fell to the floor dead. He'd had a heart attack. His father would not let the funeral home staff cut the boy's hair or put him in a fancy suit. He found that, after all, he only wanted to remember his boy the way he really was—uniquely himself.

When you are tempted to criticize or complain about your son's latest creative style of decorating himself, remember this story. For just as in a wedding, it is the odd things that happen that we laugh about, remember, and often cherish the most. (In our wedding the best man had to wear the ring bearer's tiny bow tie, and a groomsman went down the aisle in his stocking feet—he forgot to bring his shoes!) So it is the wacky things our kids did growing up that will often be the things you cherish and reminisce about in years to come.

SHOOTIN' THE BREEZE

Ask your son what the craziest thing he has ever done is. Share one or two of your crazy adventures.

Is There a Genius in Your Kitchen?

The year was 1950. A young boy wanted to make a Super-8 movie for a Boy Scout project. His mother was not the type who said, "Go outside and play; I don't want that stuff in the house." She gave him free rein of the house, letting him convert it into his film studio, moving furniture, putting backdrops over things. She bought him thirty cans of cherries and dumped them into a pressure cooker when he needed oozy red goop. She helped him make costumes and even acted in his films. Her son's name? Steven Spielberg.

One of my favorite books, a companion to a fascinating CBS special, is called *The Creative Spirit*. As the authors researched the most talented and creative minds of our century, they concluded, "In creative families there is a different feeling in the air; there's more breathing space." Breathing space. What does that mean?

JUST FOR FUN

If I could name one friend of mine who epitomizes the words *free spirit*, it would be Charlene Baumbich. I never know if Charlene will appear in a gypsy skirt with bangle earrings and a bright orange and pink scarf flowing in her hair, or dressed as a modern Pocahontas, complete with buckskin and turquoise, with her salt and pepper hair hanging softly in two braids. I love Charlene. She has breathing room, and offers it generously to all around her, beckoning, "Be yourself! Be uniquely you!"

That's why I was tickled to see that she'd written a book chock full of creative parenting ideas called *365 Ways to Connect with Your Kids—No Matter What Their Age (Or Yours)*. In her suggestion number 303, Charlene wrote, "I called to talk to a friend today who happened to have a house full of kids: her own three and several of her kids' friends. They were all laughing and carrying on in the background, busy drawing all over themselves with body paints, she said.

'What fun!' I bellowed. 'Why don't you paint yourself a tattoo on each ankle?' She thought she just might do that. And then it struck me: have a 'Family Paints the Family Night.'"

Sounds fun to me. Go for it!

It means there is room to make a mess, room to experiment, applause for successes, along with good-hearted laughter and empathy for failures. There are parents in homes with breathing space ever ready to pay a nickel for a ticket and lend enthusiastic cheers as they watch their kids' latest magic show, dance routine, or impromptu skit performed in the living room or garage. There are closets in houses with breathing room, bulging with boxes of glue, scissors, paper, glitter, and scraps of material and old magazines. There are hope chests with funny hats, old shawls, and plastic eyeglasses with noses attached waiting to be turned into costumes. Families with breathing space have minivans that turn into karaoke-mobiles on vacations to Yellowstone or Disneyland.

POINTS TO PONDER

Here are some wonderful quotes to mull over on the subject of creativity gleaned from *The Creative Spirit*. Think about these things as you encourage your son to try new tasks or to follow his unique bent or dreams.

"Creativity flourishes when things are done for enjoyment. When children learn a creative form, preserving the joy matters as much—if not more—than 'getting it right.' What matters is the pleasure, not perfection."

"Creative people often have a compelling sense of mission that drives them forward even when the odds are against them."

"Creativity entails taking appropriate risks, and courage allows you to use your intuition and will."

"Compassion, when extended to yourself, helps quiet the voice of self-judgement that discourages risk-taking."[3]

---

[3]Daniel Goleman, Paul Kaufman, and Michael Ray, *The Creative Spirit* (New York: Penguin, 1993), 38, 68–70.

There is a paradox: Although creativity takes hard work, the work goes more smoothly if you take it lightly. Humor greases the wheels of creativity.

A Boy After God's Own Heart

Read 1 Samuel 21:10–15

In this passage we see David on the run from King Saul, who now wants to kill him! David is desperate and has to use all the creativity he can just to survive. He finds food and shelter with the priest Ahimelech and then goes to King Achish of Gath.

1. Did David feel he would be safe with King Achish? Why not? (vv. 11, 12)
2. David had Goliath's sword with him, but this time, he chose not use it to fight off the bad guys. Instead he used his creative mind to get out of trouble. What crazy thing did David do to escape the dangerous city of Gath? (v. 13)

Just Do It!

Can you think of a time you used your creative mind to get yourself out of a bad or dangerous situation? Actually, policemen say that one good way to escape from a bad guy is to do something that makes you seem crazy. It sometimes confuses and surprises the criminal. David was pretty smart, eh?

A Verse in Your Pocket

God used the creative talents in David to help get him into the king's palace. As you write down or memorize this verse, notice all the ways God helped David to stand out as a special young man.

"I have seen a son of Jesse of Bethlehem who knows how to play the harp. He is a brave man and a warrior. He speaks well and is a fine-looking man. And the Lord is with him."

1 Samuel 16:18

Chapter 4

A Dozen Guys and a Mom

Encouraging Your Son's Friendships

Somewhere after five years and at least a dozen professional and personal highs and lows, my beloved literary agent, Greg Johnson, and I crossed into a friendship that embraced more than writing, more than contracts, more than either of us ever bargained for: We embraced one another's families. This meant we asked about and prayed for each other's children and spouses. I have four kids to Greg's two boys, and for some reason mine generally seem to be a lot more trouble. I'm pretty sure he's got more praying time in on my behalf than I have clocked in on his.

This past year I went through a series of nonstop crises of such proportion that at times I wondered if I could possibly withstand them emotionally or physically. (These may be revealed one day in a future book called *The Year I Survived*, but for now, trust me on this: You would feel really, really sorry for me if you had four hours to listen to me unload.) There were days all I could do was get out of bed, cry, blow my nose, and crawl back under the covers again. Most of you know what I mean, for none of us gets very far through life without a season of suffering, when we feel like a limp dishrag soaked in pain.

With each knockdown punch to what had—up until this year—been a relatively upbeat and humorous life, Greg suffered alongside every painful event that came my way. When things got really difficult, Greg's wife, Elaine, joined the prayer chain, and that's when I became the ultimate High Maintenance Author. My youngest son, Gabe, and I flew to Colorado to stay with the Johnson family in their home for several days. They had offered to give us a break, some loving company, and a little space to heal. Greg and Elaine have the sort of home that invites you to put up your feet, sigh deeply, and stretch out on the couch for a conversation, or cover up with a blanket and take a really good nap.

One thing I loved most about the Johnson home is that teenagers of all shapes and sizes wander in and out the front door as if they're in their own home, and that's exactly the way Elaine wants it. After a young teenage girl was killed in a car accident just down the street from the Johnsons' house last year, Elaine made herself a promise: She wouldn't let her sons or their friends come and leave her house without giving them a hug. Elaine is petite, not much bigger than a coffee stirrer, but she stretches up on her toes to make sure that no one—not even the six-footers—escape without their Mom Hug for the Day.

I watched Elaine dump protein powder and what seemed like half the contents of her refrigerator into an industrial-sized blender, resulting in fruity health smoothies for the noisy, happy crew gathered around the kitchen table. As she poured glasses of the cold pink shake, she teased the kids good-naturedly, exchanged sports statistics and score predictions like a pro, encouraged them in their spiritual walk, and when the house finally grew quiet, I knew she was praying for her sons, Drew and Troy, and their friends, with the earnestness of a mom who cares deeply.

The house is especially guy-friendly; even the bathrooms are decorated in sport motifs. The basement is filled with fun things for teenagers, from a pool table to a big TV with VCR, an X Box, and lots of carpet and cushions to lounge on. There's a community swimming pool nearby, a basketball court in the backyard, and a hot tub to die for next to that. Everything about the Johnsons says, "Welcome! Come on over; make yourself at home. Stay awhile and play! We're glad you are here."

Greg, Elaine, and I have seen some amazing answers to prayers concerning the lives of our kids, and we share ongoing prayer requests on a regular basis. Last week, Elaine sent this email, which warmed my heart, and left me uplifted. I hope it will encourage you too.

Hey Becky—

I wanted to share with you something cool that happened. On Friday night, I went up to our rental house in Denver with four of Drew's friends (girls this time!) to spend the night and clean the next day. I really needed their help because I neither have the time nor physical ability to do it all. So I told them I would pay them to help me. From the beginning it was so funny how they each responded like I was honoring them by inviting them. One girl was supposed to go to Boulder and get an award but wanted to go clean instead!

Anyway, we got up there, went out to dinner, and then went back to the house. I told them I wanted to talk for a few minutes if that was okay— and yes, they said, it was. Then I promised we would watch a movie, and I would go to bed and let them stay up and talk without a "mom" in the room. Well, we never got to the movie. I just shared with them my insecurities over the years and how God had done so much changing in my life this past year. I spoke the truth to them about how God loves them, they are special, each has an individual gift, and he has a perfect plan for their lives. Then so naturally I went around and spoke some truth and challenges to them each individually and differently. Then one of the girls suggested we pray!

We did, and it was such a privilege to be a part of it. We had fun and I am so grateful to be allowed to help them, hopefully, come to understand the truth about who they really are. Just think where we'd be now if we'd had someone in our lives when we were their age, huh? I knew you would think this was so cool, so I wanted to tell you. I love these kids and my boys so much that it hurts deeply to think of them having to struggle for the rest of their lives—the way I did—to be at ease with who they are in Christ. I am still of course praying for you and your family. I do believe there are miracles waiting to happen, Becky. I love you, friend.

Elaine

These are the moments that mothers pray for. This is why we put up with smelly socks and a half dozen sweaty bodies on our designer furniture as our boys and their friends drop by to watch a football game or chat. It's why we stock our fridge or fill our cookie jar with goodies to be shared, and why we put up with the extra noise and mess and trouble that comes with having a houseful.

It's because when we are old ladies sitting on our rocking chairs on the front porch, we'll remember the night we sat up late talking from our hearts about life-changing truths with a bunch of precious kids—long after the Ethan Allen furniture, tattered and stained, went for fifteen dollars in a garage sale.

(As an aside, for any of you moms who would like your husbands to read a book about raising sons—Greg has cowritten a book in this series with John Trent: *Dad's Everything Book for Sons*. I got to peek at the manuscript-in-progress and it is excellent!)

POINTS TO PONDER

Ever worry about your home being clean enough, fancy enough, large enough, for your son to be proud to have guests over? Me too—until the day my son Zeke brought home a note from a friend at school who had visited our home the weekend before. It read, "Dear Mrs. Freeman, I just want you to know I love coming to your home because there's nothin' we can do to mess it up."

Thirteen Ways to Make Your Home Kid-Friendly

1. Keep the freezer and cabinets stocked with afford-able snacks that boys tend to like. Gabe asks me to keep a box of corn dogs in the freezer, Wal-Mart soft drinks (usually under sixty cents for a two liter), and Little Debbie Snack Cakes on hand. They cheaply fill up the friends he likes to have over after a Friday night football game. I'll admit, there's a void in nutrition here, but this is "party time," and we're just trying to make the boys happy and fill 'em up for one night without breaking the bank.

2. Have kid-friendly furniture if at all possible. Soft cushy couches with washable, multicolored fabric (textured fabric shows less dirt and lasts longer) or scrubbable leather or vinyl sofas. Avoid glass topped *anything*, or fancy, delicate lamps and porcelain knickknacks. If a piece won't survive a game of living room Nerf ball or roughhousing, you're better off waiting to purchase it during that golden blip in time when your kids are out of the house and before the grandkids start to appear.

3. Greet all the kids personally as they walk in and out the door, asking them at least one question about their lives before they go home.

4. If you get to build or choose a house for raising boys— I highly suggest thinking about two stories. With the kids upstairs (and most of your living areas and mas-ter bedroom downstairs), you won't be nearly as agi-tated by the mess and noise a group of boys always generates. What you don't see won't keep you edgy.

5. Give your son's friends affectionate nicknames to make them feel a part of the family.

6. Display pictures of your son's best friends. The front of the fridge is a great place for this. Ask for a picture of them and tell them you want it to remind you to pray for them, and ask if there's anything they want you to pray about.

7. Include in the family chores your son's friends who are over often. You'll get more help, be less upset by the extra workload of having company, and they will feel like part of the family.

8. Compliment your son's friends on any achievements you've learned about or when you've caught them being good.

9. Keep your disagreements with your son private. If you are angry with him, ask him to come to another room—away from the eyes and ears of the other children—to work through any issues that are concerning you.

10. Ask a friend to go with you on a family vacation or weekend road trip. Nothing bonds a family (or sometimes, "binds and gags them") like a vacation together. We've found that letting a child's friend come along for the ride usually makes for happier kids and more fun for everyone. Plus we *really* get to know these kids after all this time together.

11. Keep a deck of cards or dominoes or other easy games handy and accessible for spontaneous play. Teach them to play a game. My mom taught our entire neighborhood of kids how to play hearts one summer.

12. Share your talents with your son and his friends. When I was a young girl growing up in the Wonder Years of the early '70s, my friend Allison had a father who was a wood craftsman by trade. One summer he made wooden "street hockey" sticks for the entire neighborhood of kids. We thought they were amazing and played hockey on our skates in the middle of the suburban cul-de-sac for days. What talent do you have that you could share with your kid's friends? Sew them a special pillow? Build them a treasure box?

13. My mother also often left a puzzle out on a folding card table during the winter months when we mostly stayed indoors. Many a relaxed conversation took place over working a jigsaw puzzle.

Creative Carpool Questions (Beyond "How Was School Today?")

1. If you are feeling sad, what meal would you want your mom to make to cheer you up?
2. If you could decorate your room again tomorrow, how would it look?
3. What was your favorite toy when you were little?
4. What are three things you like most about yourself?
5. What is one thing you'd like to change about yourself?
6. What's the best thing you remember and miss about kindergarten?

Some of these questions are taken and adapted from *201 Questions to Ask Your Kids/Parents* (Avon). It's a great little book to tuck in the glove box of your car to pull out when there's a good opportunity for talk.[4]

---

[4] Pepper Schwartz, *201 Questions to Ask Your Kids/Parents* (New York: Avon, 2000).

JUST FOR FUN

Buy Christmas stockings when they are on sale after the holidays and put the names of your son's best friends across the tops. Throughout the year collect fun, inexpensive, or free items (from Happy Meals or mail samples) and tuck them into the stockings. When Christmas comes, add a little candy and a poem, prayer, or Bible verse for them written on a card, and then give your son's friends their stockings of goodies. If you're pretty sure these friends will be around for a long time in your son's life, tell them you'll need the stockings back to fill up again next year. This way they'll know you are thinking of them all year long.

A Boy After God's Own Heart

1 Samuel 18:1–3; 20

From the moment David entered Saul's palace, Jonathan, the king's son, took an interest in this unknown shepherd boy and mentored him in the way of kings, palaces, and wars. (A mentor is an encourager and helper. He is also a friend.) In fact, the Bible says there was an immediate bond of love between them, and in time they became the best of friends.

Jonathan, no doubt, showed David how to act and serve the king in the palace and as a result, whatever Saul asked David to do, David did it successfully. But after a while, David did so well that Saul became jealous. Jonathan risked the anger of his own father to help save David's life, as you read in chapter 20.

1. Why do you think God gave David the gift of Jonathan's friendship? Do you think God knew that David was going to need a very special friend to help him when everything seemed to be going wrong?
2. What are some ways that Jonathan showed his friendship for David? (18:3, 20:12, 20:41, 42)
3. Do you have a Jonathan-friend in your life? Who is he? What are some things your Jonathan has done to help encourage you to be the best you can be?

Just Do It!

Take a minute to write a thank-you note to a special friend in your life. It will make his day!

A Verse in Your Pocket

Jonathan became one in spirit with David, and he loved him as himself.

1 SAMUEL 18:1

Chapter 5

Sports Nut Mom

Becoming a Gung-Ho Athletic Supporter

When my son Gabe and I were visiting at the Johnsons' home this year, they invited a group of folks over for The Big Basketball Game on TV. Do not ask me which big game, because I have no clue. All I know is that there had been two days of arguing between the Johnsons and their friends, the Burgers, over which team would win and the dire consequences awaiting the losers.

The men, boys, and Elaine were discussing the basketball game with foreign phrases like "flush," "pick and roll," and "rainbow from the arch." I suddenly felt as confused as I feel when talking to an auto-mechanic. Elaine tells me she feels this way at publishing dinners, so that made me feel slightly better.

Greg, seeing I was feeling a little out of my comfort zone, took me aside and said, "Beck, just go back in the living room and say, 'The refs stink!' or 'Way to shoot, Bibby!'" I practiced until I thought I had it just right and slid back into the armchair sports arena.

At what I felt was an appropriate moment of quiet, when I wouldn't interrupt anyone else, I hollered, "The refs stink! Go get 'em, Bippy!" Greg's teenage son Drew (who had only a few hours earlier asked me to take a phone number with me just in case I got lost on my walk—again) turned his head slowly in my direction and looked at me as if Ellie May Clampett had just walked in asking if anyone wanted possum for supper. With a tone usually reserved for nursery school teachers he said, "Becky, it's Bibby. Not Bippy."

"But that was pretty close," Elaine reassured.

"A good try," Greg offered.

What can I say, sports fans? Though I would dearly love to yell at the TV screen right along with the big dogs, this puppy can't ever seem to get it quite right. I've been yelling the wrong phrases at ball games for as long as my sons can remember my embarrassing them in public. I yelled, "Way to carry the ball!" at a basketball game, and "Hey! He's double dribbling on my son!" at a football game. I once sat on the wrong side of the field, cheering for my son's team all alone in a sea of confused parents. I was wondering why in the world they had lost their spirit, and they were wondering where in the world I had lost my mind. Gabe suffered a thousand deaths when I got his jersey number mixed up in my head, and cheered the wrong kid—calling him my son's name—through an entire football game. I am sorry, but in those helmets and pads, they really do look alike.

And forget about the danger for our kids playing sports. We moms (at least some of us) also risk life and limb in rooting for our sons from the sidelines. Once, visiting my son at a special Dallas Cowboy sports camp for kids, I walked across a couple of empty practice fields to get to my car. Little did I realize that the second field was anything but empty. Toting a backpack in one arm and a lawn chair under the other, I looked up in time to see a line of varsity-sized linebackers heading my way. I doubt any spectators have ever seen a middle-aged mother run across the goal line as fast, and certainly not with a lawn chair in tow.

The bleachers are no safe haven either, let me tell you. I have been inflicted with numerous welts about my head and shoulders from the hard candy the cheerleaders throw at halftime. Once, I kid you not, I was pelted in the forehead by a whole piece of pepperoni pizza that apparently flew out of nowhere. I never saw it coming. Through wind and rain and black of night, we moms trudge ever forward toward hard, cold bleachers, holding Styrofoam cups of bad coffee in one hand and an old quilt in the other. We brave the elements (including flying sourballs and pizza) for three universal purposes: to cheer should our son score a point, to console should he blow it, and to have the medical insurance card handy should he need a ride to the emergency room.

In our son Zeke's junior year, I was thankful that Scott and I were there in the stands, insurance card in hand. In the first quarter of a Friday night football game, Zeke went down on the field and did not get up. When the paramedics headed toward our son, Scott ran down the stadium steps and leaped the fence to meet them. I followed my husband as fast as I could but when I came to the fence I faced every mom's dilemma: If I climbed the fence and Zeke was okay, I knew such a scene could embarrass him for the rest of his mortal life. If, however, I didn't go out there with my son, I'd have to fight every mothering instinct that shouted, "Be with your kid!" Well, I am a mom. I climbed.

But before I reached the sidelines, Scott hollered, "Becky! He's dislocated his elbow. Now you get back over that fence and meet us at the ambulance!"

I wanted to comply, believe me.

However, at this point, I was wobbly from worry and, try as I might, could *not* get back over that fence. So the cheerleaders, taking pity on my plight, came over and did that pyramid formation stunt they do, then with a good heave-ho, pushed me over the fence. Upon landing on my kneecaps, I could not get up. Two men came to my rescue and had to half-carry, half-walk me to my car. One of them, as gently as possible, pointed out the fact that there was a gate not five feet from where I had fallen.

When I arrived at the hospital and the feeling returned to my legs, I limped over to my poor son who was lying in pain, his arm outstretched in a sling before him. I kissed his forehead and he tenderly reassured me. "Mom, it's okay. God was with me." Then, his voice turned suddenly stern. "And, Mom, don't you *ever* think of doing that again."

The Care and Feeding of Your Young Athlete

Our boys, after working out at the school gym or daily after-school practices, need the right foods to support their health. Beyond what most moms know about nutrition and the food pyramid, kids who are involved in strenuous athletics may need to consume more food, at regular intervals, and breakfast is a must. Fruits and veggies are great. (See Elaine's Power Shake recipe below if your guys are reluctant to eat these.) Carbs such as pasta, rice, cereal, oatmeal, and whole grain breads are like gasoline for the body and without them your little athlete is running on empty.

A side benefit of your child's involvement with sports is that his desire to perform well as an athlete may motivate him to eat healthy for the first time. Instead of saying, "Come on, eat your carrots, they are *good* for you," you can honestly say, "If you want to play your best game on Friday, you gotta put the right fuel in your body."

Kids need about forty different nutrients and the easiest way to help them get their vitamins and minerals is to provide them with a variety of colors in their food choices. A colorful fruit or veggie tray with fun dips are perfect snacks for the whole family.

JUST FOR FUN

For those of you moms who, like me, would like to impress your living room sports' fans with some new basketball trivia and lingo—Greg Johnson agreed to the following brief interview to help us out.

Me: So Greg, what is Bibby's last name?

Greg: Bibby.

Me: Oookay. Let's try that again. What's his whole name?

Greg: Mike Bibby.

Me: What team does he play for?

Greg: Sacramento Kings.

Me: Tell me, what does *flush* mean, besides something guys often forget to do.

Greg: *Flush* means to dunk the ball with authority

Me: What about *pick and roll*—beyond what boys do with their dirty T-shirts before they *flush* them in the hamper with authority?

Greg: A *pick and roll* is a screen and cutaway maneuver between two people.

Me: Well, I'm glad you've cleared up my confusion on that one. (Translation: I am too embarrassed to follow up this question with "What the heck is a screen and cutaway maneuver?" I have my pride.) And what is a *rainbow from beyond the arc*?

Greg: It's a three-pointer far out from the line that has a high arc.

Me: I actually understand this one! It's going to be my new, most favorite basketball term.

Greg: I can't wait to hear you use it in context. I could use the material for my book.

Drink Up!

Your child should drink water or other fluids throughout the day but especially during and after periods of physical activity, about one cup for every half-hour to an hour of activity is a good rule of thumb. With recent tragedies of professional athletes dying on the field from dehydration and heatstroke, parents have good reason to emphasize the importance of hydration—especially on hot summer days.

Children often fail to recognize or respond to feelings of thirst. The coach or assistant should know this and encourage the kids to drink even before they feel thirsty. Tell your son to check the color of his urine: If it is clear or the color of pale lemonade, he is getting enough water.

If it is dark, like the color of apple juice, however, he may be on the way to heatstroke.

Although many sports drinks are available, plain water is usually what kids need. Sports drinks advertise that they replace electrolytes such as the sodium and potassium lost in sweat. But in most cases, lost electrolytes can be replenished by a good meal after the activity. Endurance-sport participants are the exception. If your child is involved in intense exertion for more than two hours, some type of sports drink may be beneficial for replenishing carbohydrates. This is because the sugar (a simple carbohydrate) found in such drinks can serve as a temporary replacement for complex carbohydrates, assuming your child eats well before and after the activity.

Weighty Matters

Some school-age athletes face unique pressures involving nutrition and body weight. In sports such as football, kids may feel they need to radically increase body weight. In other sports such as wrestling, young athletes may try to spit, vomit, or sweat enough water from their bodies to qualify for the lowest possible weight class. In the long run they are hurting themselves. Muscles are 75 percent water, and if water is compromised for weight loss, strength will soon disappear as well. With super-fast weight gain, the pounds are often stored as fat instead of muscle, again sacrificing strength and health to meet a desired number on a scale.

Game Day

Your child should eat well on game days, but make sure he eats early enough so that there's time to digest before game time. For a full meal, that usually means two to three hours before the event. The meal itself should not be very different from what your child has been eating throughout his training. It's a cumulative process, and your son can't expect to eat well only on game days and be at his best. However, game-day meals should be based on complex carbs with less fat and protein (since these take longer to digest). The closer to game time, it's best not to take in much food. A good meal after the game, with protein and some fat and carbs replenishes their bodies. And again, he'll need a lot of water or a sports drink.

Meals of Champions—Quick Healthy Suggestions

Breakfast
- Yogurt parfait, layered with some granola and a banana
- Nutritious cereal or oatmeal, a glass of milk and some fruit

Lunch
- Tuna sandwiches on whole grain bread (or whole grain crackers) with veggies
- Bean burritos with some low-fat cheese, lettuce, and tomatoes

Dinner
- Grilled chicken breasts with steamed rice and vegetables
- Baked or grilled fish, veggies and baked potato

Snacks
- Pretzels
- Fresh or dried fruit
- Fruit and protein shakes
- Veggie trays

Elaine's Power Shake Recipe
Mix 4 cups of any fruit—seeded and chopped in big chunks

(I try to use at least one banana for sweetness)
1 cup fruit juice, water, yogurt, or milk
Scoop of protein powder
Put in vitamix and blend.
(You can order these power mixers at www.vitamix.com)

POINTS TO PONDER

Everything to do with a sporting event confuses me, even the bathrooms. Both the men's and the women's doors, for starters, look exactly alike at most stadiums. During one high school halftime, I mistakenly entered the men's restroom, unnerving more than a few unzipped fellows. Mortified, I quickly escaped and ducked into the door a few feet away—only to discover the same panicked expression on the same familiar faces. Turns out there were two doors to the men's room, an entrance and an exit, and I'd managed to grace them both in less than thirty seconds.

How do you handle your embarrassing moments? Someone once said, "You grow up the first time you have a good laugh at yourself." Might as well get a head start on growing up and get in the habit of not taking yourself too seriously. It's a lot more fun. And you'll be passing on the gift of humor to your son, which is no small survival tool for most of us.

Training at Home

My husband, Scott, did not play any organized sports after eighth grade—by choice. I never played any organized sports due to lack of interest and ability. (I was voted Most Feminine in my junior high gym class because they couldn't think of an honest athletic honor to give me.)

Neither of us are shining examples of team players; we know little about football, basketball, soccer, and baseball; and, yet, we love to watch our kids play sports. To our great amazement, they are quite good! In fact, our youngest son, Gabe, will be the starting running back for the varsity team this fall, and he scored the only touchdown in the last varsity play-off game last season as a freshman.

So, moms, fear not if you or your husband stink at organized team sports. It does not mean that your kids are destined to warm the bench for the length of their school days.

Your sons will be delighted if you just get out in the backyard and make a fool of yourself playing one-on-one, letting them run over you in touch football, or hit an over-the-fence ball from your lousy pitches. Show enthusiasm at practices, cheer at games, join the athletic booster club, and clip out the local newspaper game summaries if ever your child's name or picture appears. (Win their hearts by starting a sports scrapbook in their honor!)

If at all possible make your yard sports friendly. We have some friends who are moving to a home on more acreage down the street from where they currently live, because their boys love baseball (as do the neighborhood kids) and want room for their own baseball field. A slab of concrete (or hard-packed dirt) and a basketball hoop is a kid magnet. And poles stuck in concrete-filled tires with a high-quality volleyball net strung between them will guarantee many hours of family, neighborhood, and youth group fun.

Coaches

Good coaches are like gold. Your boys will probably have a mixture of the good, the bad, and the ugly in terms of school coaches throughout their years. Unless the coaches become abusive or single your son out in humiliating ways, it is generally best to bite your tongue, Mom, and encourage your boy to be respectful (and bite his tongue), to say, "Yes sir," and get back into the game. It's so hard, I know, to watch our sons from the sidelines in silence at times. But team sports are a microcosm of real life—and life is full of situations where we have to deal with authority, accept correction we feel is unfair at times, and play as a member of a team without hogging the limelight or mouthing off at the ref. If the situation grows obviously demeaning to your son and he has done everything he knows to be respectful, play hard, and show up on time, male coaches almost always react more positively (sexist though it may be) to your husband (or another calm man in your family) coming to talk about the problem, than they do to us moms marching into their office (or God forbid, on the field!) to defend our little boy.

Becoming a Good Sport

Not always, but often, the best natural athletes, the most aggressive and fearless players will have the hardest time controlling their temper on the field or court. They demand so much of themselves—or their teammates—that the frustration mixed with the TNT of testosterone can prove explosive. This is when tough love has to prevail, and your son needs it from all directions: you, your husband, and his coaches. With time and consistency, and lots of encouragement when he shows self-control in a frustrating situation, your son will eventually realize that no matter how much talent he has (or doesn't have), the joy of the game will disappear if he doesn't get a grip.

This is a great time to watch classic sports movies together to point out the calm, controlled power that enduring athletes—those who are most respected—always exhibit. The best athletes play smarter, not harder—saving their energy for the game. They know they can't afford to let any of it leak out over a poor call from a ref or a foul from the opposing team. The best "revenge" is always a game well played, even if it ends in a losing score.

I often tell son Gabe before a game my own version of the famous line from *Chariots of Fire:* "Gabe, go out there and feel God's pleasure when you run." If our kids lose the sense of fun, of God's pleasure at their performance, sports can become a cruel taskmaster, an arena where they feel they are never quite good enough rather than the high energy school of wisdom it can become.

When my boys first wanted to play football, I worried a lot about their physical safety (still do!), but my gentle father (who is much more of a leisurely golfer and fisherman than a football fan) told me something that eased my mind. "Becky, let them play. You can do all you can to see that safety measures are taken, but ultimately there are things your sons will learn on a team that they will need to grow into manhood well. Things like taking risks, playing hard, practicing for a future goal, working as a team, giving something your all, overcoming odds, respecting authority even when they push you to your limits, self-control, accepting defeat graciously because there's always another game, and the pure joy of a hard-earned win."

After watching three sons experience the tragedy and triumph of playing sports, I have to say that my father was right. Perhaps the most poignant athletic triumph of all occurred during Zeke's senior year. During the second game of the season, once again, Zeke went down on the field—and dislocated his *other* elbow. This time I didn't climb the fence, but my heart broke not only for the pain he was in, physically, but the enormous sadness he would face at being put out of the games for an injury again—and this was his last year of high school. I watched as he stood on the sidelines in games that followed, his muscles straining to be with the team, and one time I saw his Adam's apple move up and down his skinny neck, knowing he was swallowing tears, so badly did he want to be out there with his teammates.

Even with a dislocated elbow, Zeke kept practicing, holding his arm as he ran around the track to stay in shape while his teammates practiced in the middle of the field. He worked diligently at physical therapy until he was finally allowed to play again, and he gave the last two games of the season every ounce of energy he had.

At the end of the year his coach walked up to a podium at a local sports banquet and said, "We coaches only give one award each year, and it goes to a player who shows us that in spite of perplexing, defeating odds, with the last ounce of strength he has, gets up, gets back in the game, and plays with all his heart for the team he loves. This year the Fighting Heart Award goes to Zeke Freeman."

Well, I'm a mom. I cried.

To this day, I see Zeke taking what he learned in team sports—about overcoming defeat graciously, persisting until he made his goals, and enjoying the fruits of victory in his beautiful life, lived to the hilt, as a young man sold out to God.

What if My Son Is *Not* a Natural Athlete?

We have three sons in our family and each of them is gifted very different physically. Gabe, our youngest, is truly the only son who is perfectly designed for team sports. This kid had a V-shaped chest, a "six-pack" stomach, and bulging muscles by the time he was eleven years old, much to the consternation of his two older brothers. He began playing the coveted position of running back on the varsity team toward the end of his freshman year. Gabe's a natural at football and basketball, which happen to be the two most popular sports in our small town in Texas. My sister, Rachel, once commented on Gabe's amazing physique and in a Dr. Frankenstein accent said, "Becky, you finally created the *perfect human*." So, basically, Gabe drew the best cards from our gene pool in terms of playing school sports.

Our oldest son, Zachary, went through a long and painful chubby stage that lasted, bless his heart, from seventh through twelfth grades. He suddenly and permanently trimmed down the summer he graduated from high school. We could see early on that playing team sports frustrated more than encouraged Zach, so we encouraged, but never pressured him to play. He turned in his jerseys during his junior year and set his sights on other sports. Zach became the best hunter and fisherman of the family, loving his time in the woods and on the lake with a couple of other good buddies. (I always mentally whistled the theme song from *The Andy Griffith Show* every time I watched him walk toward the woods with a fishing pole slung over his shoulder.) He was the grandson who took up golf, much to my golfing father's delight, and he was our only child who ever bought a horse and took up horseback riding. In college, Zach loved to snorkel around the clear rivers in south Texas and took up Frisbee golf with a passion.

Zeke played football and loved it, though he was not naturally built for the rigors of the sport—and his tall, thin body took a lot of punishment, as you've previously read. Zeke and his father took to rock climbing, however, as if they were born for the sport. Agile and light, Zeke also excelled at cycling and running. In college he ran triathlons and did very well. He can also windsurf and water-ski with amazing grace.

All of this is to say, if your son doesn't happen to have what it takes to be a quarterback or point guard, remember that there's a whole world of sports beyond the typical school teams. Encourage him to try a wide variety of activities, to explore anything physical that will keep his body moving and encourage both fun and fitness.

Even the most unathletic males among us—those who prefer band instruments to weight lifting, or poetry to push-ups—can find some sort of physical activity that will enrich their lives and their health.

A Boy After God's Own Heart

2 Samuel 22:29–37

This is part of David's long song of praise (a "psalm") after God had given him victory in many battles. Read this portion of the song where David gives God all the glory for his physical strength and abilities, then fill in the blanks:

You are my _____ , O Lord,
The Lord turns my darkness into _____.
With your help I can _____ against a _____.
With my God I can _____ a wall.
It is God who arms me with _____
And makes my way perfect.
He makes my feet like _____;
He enables me to stand on the heights.
He trains my _____ for battle.
My arms can _____a bow of bronze.
You give me your shield of _____;
You stoop down to make me _____.
You broaden the _____ beneath me,
So that my _____ do not turn.

Just Do It!

Now think of the ways God gives you strength to play a sport or participate physically in outdoor activities. Write your own song (or a psalm) about it as David did and use it as a prayer before you do something challenging or athletic.

Keep a Verse in Your Pocket

Memorize the last part of this verse:

With my God I can scale a wall.

2 SAMUEL 22:30

Chapter 6

Where Did My Little Boy Go?

Navigating the Adolescent Freeway

It came as such a shock when my oldest son, Zachary, turned thirteen. Ready or not, we were entering the teenage zone—the stage when adolescents have more hormones than brains.

One morning as I was about to exit the driveway with a car full of kids and head to their school, I realized I had forgotten to eat breakfast. I stopped the car and asked Zach to run in the house and get me a banana.

The next thing I knew he was running toward the house with his arms flattened against his ribs and his head cocked to one side. Then he turned around and ran back to the car in the same peculiar way—without having procured the banana.

"Son! What are you doing?" I demanded. He looked at me with sincere surprise.

"Didn't you tell me to run to the house and back, like a banana?"

This was my first hint that we might be approaching the classic mom/teen communication gap.

Gabe's girlfriend, Allison, who just turned sixteen, is, well, *a lot* like me when I was sixteen: naïve as a young goose in a new world. She recently tried to fax Gabe a letter—while it was still folded inside an envelope. I guess she thought somehow the letter would float out of the envelope and appear magically on our fax machine. Don't ponder it too long; your head will begin to hurt if you try to follow the logic.

Thirteen was tough, but when Zach turned sixteen I had a hard time just saying the number out loud in connection with his age. The age of sixteen, as you know, traditionally ushers in a new driver, which, at least in our case, also ushered in a hysterically nervous mother with her foot firmly embedded in the passenger-side floorboard.

Gabe will be sixteen next month. He recently got his driver's permit and could not wait for his turn at the wheel. I reluctantly took my place on the right side of the front seat and dug my fingernails into the armrests, right foot into the floorboard, in anticipation. He drove exactly two feet in our driveway before I screamed, "STOP! You're in DRIVE instead of REVERSE!"

Gabe promptly stopped the car, put it in park, and said, "I'm never driving with you again. Ever." And I said exactly the same thing back to him, and delegated driver's training to his father from this point on. A mother shouldn't have to go through this sort of nerve-racking torture more than three times in her adult life. I believe my last driver's training nerve was shot when my daughter jumped a curb just before I gave up driving with her too. I'm the world's worst driver, anyway. Why would society want me to teach anyone else how to navigate public roads?

Another right of passage from childhood to adulthood associated with the number 16 turned out to be more like a riot of passage with Zachary.

I'll never forget the afternoon Zach's boss called from the gas station where he secured his first job to warn us our son would be coming home early. "Now, don't be too shocked when you first see him. It's not as bad as it looks."

I sat on the back porch puzzling over what this might mean, when my teenager rounded the bend and my mouth dropped open. Zach was literally covered from head to foot with great globs of dripping black grease. He looked like a toxic waste dump in Nike tennis shoes. His dad handed him a bucket of grease remover, and after he had cleaned up the worst of it, the story unfolded.

A customer had pulled up to the station and asked Zach to put a couple of quarts of oil in his car. Zach cheerfully agreed to the task. When the man came out of the store and saw what Zach was doing (which was in truth, simply following orders) the man yelled, "Son, you didn't put all of the two quarts of oil in there, did you?" Puzzled by the man's rage, Zach answered. "Yes sir, I did."

"Well," ranted the irate customer, "you've got to get under there and take out the plug and let some of it out right now. You overfilled it."

Zach, being young and still of a mind to try to please the man, obliged. It might have worked, had the plug not broken loose while Zach was twisting it off the bottom of the oil pan. As things were, Zach ended up on the receiving end of an oil bath. (Only a few weeks earlier, Zach had accidentally poured a quart of oil in a customer's radiator.)

The next morning I received another call from Zach's boss. Thankfully, she was laughing. "Becky," she said, "you haven't finished the chapter on Zach, have you? Because I've got another good one for you."

"What happened now?" I asked, grabbing for a pen and paper. Zach had accidentally left his application for a D-FY-IT card at the store. A D-FY-IT card is a discount card the kids in our local school district can receive if they pass a drug test and promise to stay drug-free. The questionnaire asked for the students to describe any prescriptions or over-the-counter pharmaceutical products they may have taken in the last twenty-four hours. Zachary, wanting so badly to be conscientious made sure he'd covered all the bases. His drug list? Aspirin, Crest, Speed Stick deodorant, and Barbasol shaving cream.

I couldn't help laughing. I could just see some police officer chuckling, "Son, when was the last time you got high on toothpaste?" or even better, "I'm sorry, Mr. Freeman, but I'm going to have to book you for possession of deodorant."

Driving, jobs, hair, hormones, *girls!* It's all ahead of you, Mom. Beyond a hearty sense of humor, buckled in with a seat belt of prayer, how can you prepare for the bumpy ride ahead?

What's Happenin', Man?

Annette Smith, registered nurse, friend, and author of *Help! My Little Boy's Growing Up!* has some wonderful comments about the season of puberty in our son's lives.

The changes that you are seeing now—or that you will soon see—are occurring exactly the way God planned. His design is perfect. Though it may appear that hormones have caused your son to go haywire, an adolescent boy's body is not broken. It does not need to be fixed. These are exciting years, because it's now that we begin to see a glimmer of the man our son is going to be.

Annette also says that boys need information as their bodies change. They have questions and wonder if they are normal. With her great southern-style sense of humor, Annette says, "Most moms can get away with addressing basic gender-neutral topics like voice changes, body odor, and acne, but nearly all boys most emphatically do not care to discuss with their mother any of those matters taking place further south than their armpits." [5]

Dad is the most natural person to discuss the topics of puberty and sex with your son, but sometimes a father is either unavailable or not up to the task. In this case, you may need to arrange for someone who already spends a good deal of time with your son to talk to him—a grandfather, uncle, trusted family friend, or a big brother, if he is mature and believes in moral purity.

Brief Review of the Facts of Life

1. Sometime between the ages of ten and fourteen, the pituitary gland sets in motion events that boost testosterone, triggering all sorts of changes. It will be between ages sixteen and eighteen that this process is complete.

---

[5] Annette Smith, *Help! My Little Boy's Growing Up* (Eugene, OR: Harvest House, 2002), 21–31.

2. Life is hardest on the boys who are late bloomers. Another man who was a late bloomer can encourage your son if he is a little behind the other boys in growth.

3. The average adolescent boy will nearly double his weight between the ages of twelve and sixteen. His height may increase four or more inches in a year (and your grocery bill will increase accordingly!).

4. Sweat glands become active and you may have to be a little more firm about the need for showers. Purchase him some nice-smelling manly deodorant and cologne to encourage him to stay fragrant. Also keep baking powder handy for him to sprinkle in his shoes. I have nearly fainted, dead-away, from the smell of adolescent boys' shoes throughout my years of mothering.

5. Though you probably don't want to think about it, this is the age when hair appears—everywhere—and if that's not enough to make you nervous, by this point he will probably experience nocturnal emissions or "wet dreams." Annette says it's a good idea to teach your son to do his own laundry occasionally before puberty, so "if the need arises" he can launder his own sheets or underwear without calling unwanted attention to what, for him, will be an embarrassing situation. Respecting his privacy is going to be increasingly important.

6. Masturbation, according to Dr. James Dobson, is one of those things that nearly 100 percent of boys will do. Though you may disagree, I personally believe that it's something we don't need to make our sons feel guilty about. In fact, most Christian counselors

would agree that masturbation is a God-given release to help a celibate young man get through the temptation of having early sexual encounters with girls. Obsessive sexual problems usually don't arise unless there is access to pornography. The open access to porn through the easy availability of Internet and cable TV in homes is like opening a candy store for a diabetic. Use parental controls. Check the "history" of your computer now and then. If the rules are being violated, better to restrict or even get rid of the Internet access and cable channels than put your son within reach of too much temptation. Fleeing temptation is often the best option for avoiding sin.

JUST FOR FUN!

When a shadow first appears on your son's upper lip, let him go shopping with you to pick out shaving cream, a good razor, and some aftershave that will make him feel like real man!

When Girls Stop Being Yucky

It will be normal for your son to have infatuations or even crushes on girls at this time. Before the time for dating happens, it's a good idea to decide your family policies on dating a couple of years in advance.

Here's a sample of the Smith Family Dating Rules from Annette's book.

1. No individual "car" dates before age sixteen.
2. We must know where you will be at all times. If your plans change or you will be home later than the time

we've agreed upon, we expect a call. (I'd add that a call also needs to be made to the girl's parents.)

3. No dating anyone more than two grades ahead or two grades behind.

4. No more than one "alone" date per week. Church activities, group dates, and parties are not included.

5. You may go to a girl's house or she may visit in our home one evening a week, but only if a parent is present in the house.

Annette says these rules can be bent when circumstances seem to merit doing so, and that your family has to decide what is best and works for you.

I've found that long nightly phone calls can get to be a problem, as well as hours of emailing during the pre-dating years. If the situation gets out of hand, limit the time allowed for talking on the phone or emailing. You may have to get a timer. I know that emailing for me can almost become addicting. It's like the excitement of getting a letter, but it can happen several times a day. If we as adults have problems controlling our time, you know our kids will struggle as well. Give them a little help.

SHOOTIN' THE BREEZE

Ask your son who his best girl friend is—not as a romantic interest, but as just a really good girl buddy. Talk about some of the good male friends you had when you were younger and why you liked them.

Positive Guy-Girl Friendships

We rarely hear about the value of good, platonic friendships between boys and girls—usually just warnings about keeping them away from sexual experimentation. But cross-gender friendships can be a great, positive enhancement to your son's life as he grows up.

According to researcher William Pollack,

> For many boys, especially boys younger than fourteen years of age, girls as friends means sharing respectful, fun-oriented experiences that generally involve only limited talking, with this talking focused primarily on shared interests and struggles with parents. For other boys, usually older, having a girl as a friend offers an opportunity for intimate verbal connection and deep emotional support freed from the struggles of romantic demands and sexual nuances.[6]

Gabe has a friend, Sarah, who is more like a sister than a friend. She lives only two doors down from us and the two of them talk and play basketball and ski around the lake in the summertime and have enjoyed each other's company for years—but both of them make the gagging symbol when their friends suggest they should become boyfriend and girlfriend. Sometimes they even fight like brother and sister, with opinionated Gabe and strong-willed Sarah going at it in an argument, but always making up. Her mother, Melissa, and I think their relationship is a joy to behold. It's healthy and helpful to both of them.

It has been found that good, healthy guy-girl friendships allow a boy a little time off from having to be the standard macho male—and experience at least fleeting moments of liberation when it's safe to break the rules

---

[6] William Pollack, *Real Boys* (New York: Random House, 1998).

and just be himself. I've noticed, simply from observation, that in very small school classes there seems to be more of this guy-girl friendship. One girl explained to me, "When you grow up with the same twenty or thirty kids from kindergarten, it's more like a big group of friends. I guess there's not much mystery after spending so much time and so many years together, and romantic crushes tend to happen outside of our group."

> POINTS TO PONDER
>
> "Over the past few years, I've developed friendships with girls. Girls give you a different point of view than a guy. They sometimes can be more sensitive with advice. When a guy gives you advice you get one half of the picture and when a girl gives you advice you get the other half of the picture. When you get advice from both sides you get the whole picture."
> —Patrick, age sixteen
>
> "We both like watching fun movies, so she comes over and watches them a lot. We like the same type of music. She is just one of the guys, basically."
> —Robert, age ten[7]

Gallantry Rediscovered

I believe the best things we can do for our sons are to teach them to value girls highly and what it means to treat them as young ladies, especially before they go on their first date. These things include how to ask her out politely, talk to her parents, look the father in the eye, walk to the door, open the doors, pay for her dinner, walk

---

[7]Pollack, *Real Boys*, 202.

her back to the door, bring her home on time, etc. I just watched a movie, *Kate and Leopold*, about a nineteenth-century gentlemen who time-traveled to our modern era, meeting a career-wise, tough-talking woman, played by Meg Ryan. What fascinated me was the way Leopold was trained to honor and revere a woman, protecting her from men with questionable intentions, rising at the table when she left and entered a room. It was also interesting how Kate loved being treated with respect, like a real lady.

What happened to gallantry? When did raw, naked sex replace the mystery of a beautiful romance on the silver screen? It's important to expose your sons to times when gallantry was alive through movies and books. As much as they may balk at first, try playing some of those great old movies on a lazy Saturday or Sunday afternoon. Movies where men treated women like ladies to be courted, and not like objects for the next romp in the hay. One of my favorite old musicals is *Seven Brides for Seven Brothers*, where brothers, who are raised wild and without a mother's care, are taught how to treat young women as the ladies they are.

JUST FOR FUN!

Buy or rent the movie *A Walk to Remember*. It is one of the best movies I've seen that teaches a boy about the sort of girl he will probably want to look for and eventually marry someday. I've observed Gabe and many of his guy friends talking about this movie, overhearing them say that this is the sort of relationship they want someday. So few well-done Hollywood-produced movies have standards this high these days, and treat Christians with such gentle respect.

A Boy After God's Own Heart

Read 1 Samuel 25

In this chapter we read about David, who is reacting to a selfish, fool of a man named Nabal by getting angry himself, so angry, in fact, that he is ready to kill! Then enters beautiful, intelligent Abigail—a woman who is head and shoulders above her husband in wisdom.

Because of Abigail's insight, she reminds David that his life belongs to the Lord, who promises to sling out his enemies for him, "as if from the hollow of a sling." Abigail probably heard of David's slaying of Goliath with his sling, and now she reminds David that the victory was his long ago—because he asked for God's help. In this case against Nabal, David is just thirsty for revenge. It's nothing but macho pride. David has not prayed about what he is going to do, and Abigail urges him to behave like the great king of Israel that he is, to seek God's help before he does anything rash.

1. What sort of woman was Abigail? (v. 3)
2. What would have happened if Abigail had not obeyed the Lord and met David to try to talk him out of his plan? (v. 34)
3. What did David decide to do instead? (v. 35)
4. What happened to Nabal? (vv. 36–38)
5. What did David say and do next? (v. 39)

Abigail was a beautiful woman with a good head on her shoulders, and she wasn't afraid to give the king good advice. He took it and saved himself from starting another war, a war that he hadn't even prayed about entering. Someday, a long time from now, when you decide whom to marry, you may want to remember this story of Abigail and ask God to give you a wife like her!

Just Do It!

Abigail means "my Father's joy"—one who gives joy to others. Do you know any girls like Abigail? Any teenagers or women like her? What girl would you go to for advice if you had a problem and could not go to an adult or a guy friend?

A Verse in Your Pocket

Praise be to the Lord, the God of Israel, who has sent you today to meet me. May you be blessed for your good judgment.

1 SAMUEL 25:32–33

Chapter 7

Every Son, a Hero

*Instilling a Grand Sense of Purpose
in Your Son's Heart*

One of the best books written for men that I, as a
card-carrying female, have sneaked past the covers to read is *Wild at Heart* by John Eldridge. If you
want to get into the minds of your sons and husbands—or
any of the men in your life, grab a copy of this book, and be
prepared to think like a guy. (You might want to belch
loudly to help set a scene filled with masculine mystique.)

One of the most important points that Eldridge makes
is that every male needs three things to live a meaningful,
purposeful life:

1. A battle to fight
2. A maiden to rescue
3. A dragon to slay

A man, or a boy, who does not see himself as a potential hero in the drama of life, who does not have the sense that he is on a sacred quest, will live his life on the sidelines or search for addictions to fill the void. Keeping our kids away from drugs won't be nearly as difficult if life itself is the ultimate trip.

Our sons must catch the vision that life is an adventure to be lived, and that he is meant to be involved in a quest far greater than himself. Our little boys, playing the action-figure-hero games of the day, are just miniature Don Quixotes in search of a mission that will require courage, honor, and gallantry. It is no wonder that when thoroughly modern men are asked "What is the best movie you've ever seen?" most of them will reply *Braveheart* or *Gladiator,* both movies about noble dreams from long-ago days, and sacred sacrifices for the good of others.

As a queasy tenderfoot mom, I have to admit to never having actually seen *Braveheart* or *Gladiator,* but I've heard descriptions over dinner conversations that sometimes sent me reeling to the restroom. I do not understand a man's general toleration for violence and blood, however honorably shed, but I do understand that these are films fathers want to see with their sons, and both come away with a misty-eyed sense of rediscovered honor. They've seen a glimpse of the sort of man they would like to be, a legacy they'd like to leave. There's a seed in every boy that would like to know that he, if called upon, could lay down his life for God, family, and country. And that there is a fight for the right that calls a man to disregard comfort, complacency, and safety, for the joy of losing himself in a greater cause.

A little while ago I was speaking in Oklahoma City and toured the Murray Building Memorial on September

11, the one-year anniversary of the 9-11 attack. On that poignant day, all of the pictures, sounds, and stories from both the bombing in Oklahoma and the plane attacks in New York City pointed not only to evil, but to one other unavoidable fact: Men are at their brilliant best when called upon to be heroes. Not only did we see business-men transform into the bravest of soldiers aboard the doomed planes, we saw firefighters walk into infernos of death to save their fellow men, and rescue workers will-ing to push their bodies beyond normal physical limits in hopes of saving just one life from the wreckage. We saw ordinary men become the greatest versions of themselves, and a country—now fused with a mission of honor—rise to its feet and salute these national heroes with a fervency not seen before in our heretofore me-first generation.

So, moms, how can we encourage our boys toward glo-rious quests and the assurance that their part in a mission, God's plan, is essential? How do we help them see that without their God-ordained input in the world, it will be a lesser place?

I once read that the greatest thing Jesus did was go around touching people and saying, "You are needed" by asking people to follow him, learn from him, and then spread that message to others in need of God's love. He provided examples, like the Good Samaritan and the poor widow who gave what they could to help others. The thought that our input into other lives matters to God, indeed, seems to call out the best in humankind. It's our duty as moms to convey this vital message to our sons.

Storybook Mentors

I believe one of the most important classic tales for young men to hear is the story of King Arthur's Camelot.

Not only is it an exciting read, but like most enduring literature, the spiritual parallels are compelling. *First Knight* is an excellent movie version of the Camelot story, where we see not only the pull of temptation in Guinevere and Lancelot, but also the hurt that their ultimate betrayal and sin causes King Arthur (who I believe is often a Christ figure in this tale). Camelot, that shining city on a hill, will fall most surely because of a man and woman's sin, of their giving in to lust at the price of a kingdom. If it were not for Arthur's ultimate sacrifice on behalf of his beloved betrayers, all would have been lost. We can see allegorical glimpses of Adam and Eve's betrayal, Eden lost, and Christ's heartache at the great fall, followed by forgiveness and the sacrifice of his own life to save humankind and the kingdom of God. Not only does the story of Arthur and his Round Table point out spiritual truths, but Arthur himself makes a great storybook mentor for boys.

Max, a man who grew up in a series of foster families that were often violent, found that his one joy in life was reading. Today Max is a senior VP of a major corporation and is known as a wise, generous employee-centered leader. So how did Max get from Point A (child of unwed teens from a poor family) to Point B (much-admired leader of a large organization)?

In the book *How We Choose to Be Happy*, the authors interviewed Max, who had an epiphany at age eleven. In the interview Max said,

> Though it happened forty years ago, I remember the day as though it were yesterday. In school we were required to read *King Arthur and His Knights of the Round Table*. Arthur's kingdom was a won-

derful world in which people intended to be honorable and trustworthy and good. In this kingdom people treated each other well and respected one another. Arthur had created such a happy place. I fell in love with his kingdom.

Then Max made the leap from the pages of the book to his own young heart. "I remember the moment when I thought to myself, 'I can do this. I will lead my life as King Arthur led his.' I had little in the way of value systems at that time and this seemed like such an ideal world."

Having no money to buy the book for himself, Max smuggled it out of the classroom and took it home to reread late at night, committing parts of it to memory. (I know, it's ironic that he stole a book in order to learn about virtue, but God always begins with us where we are.) It became his map to a better world.

"Believe it or not," the fifty-two-year-old Max said, "King Arthur has been my guiding light ever since. He was really a people builder. . . . I've chosen to live my life using what I learned from that book for over forty years and it still makes me happy."

Why is this true? Perhaps Max hit the nail on the knighted head. In King Arthur's Camelot there are plenty of dragons to fight, maidens to rescue, and battles to win. In the same way, the Bible offers just such a sense of adventure to young boys. We have Satan, that old dragon, and his evil to fight. We have battles to overcome—obstacles of life that challenge our faith. And there are maidens to rescue—others in need of the saving grace Christ brings, news we can share to pull them out of the dark dungeons and into his brilliant light.

This is one of the reasons I've chosen to use the life of King David throughout this book for the Bible study portions. We have action, battles, intrigue, honor, the loss of honor, mercy, and restoration. We have the stuff adventures are made of!

No More Ordinary Days

So, moms, not only do we want to let our sons know they are needed, but we also need to find ways to convey that the Christian life is anything but boring. I'm reading a book by Joy Dawson right now with a fabulous title: *Forever Ruined for the Ordinary*. It's about intimacy and communication with God in a moment-by-moment walk of life, asking him questions and learning how to listen for his answers. He really does speak to us individually every day. The question is, are we listening? Do we even know how to listen?

Many days I just live and move through time, unaware of God's communication to me, almost sleepwalking through the hours. But when I wake up spiritually and tune in to the channel of prayer and awareness of him, even the most mundane experiences take on a holy glow.

I talked with an energetic woman yesterday. She owns a local boutique and is a perfect example of a Christian who is awake and aware. There was something remarkable about her and I knew it almost immediately. She was actively sensitive to God's Spirit (without being pushy or weird about it), and saw her customers and her work as a privilege, as holy work. As we visited, she told me she took a trip alone and drove for ten hours straight. Before I could groan about the long distance, she continued her story with enthusiasm. "Ten hours! Can you believe it? Ten hours alone to talk with

God and listen to him speak to my heart. It was glorious. I could have driven forever." This lady has been forever ruined for the ordinary. Her children, if they catch their mother's secret of joy and purpose, are blessed indeed.

I have a personal theory that the popularity of the book *The Prayer of Jabez* and the Bible studies series *Experiencing God* has a common thread: Both authors of both books confirm the exciting thought that God is very interested in us personally. As we learn to hear his voice and follow it in faith, he will use us as a vessel of his love to the world in amazing, miraculous ways. The realization that God wants to communicate with us in a variety of creative ways is the difference between living a dull life of religion and waking up excited to read the scriptures and pray, awaiting our "marching orders" for the day, as it were.

If we, as moms, learn to listen to the King of Kings' voice, to know when he is urging us to follow into the next adventure, and the next, and the next, life will be anything but routine. If you want to instill a lifelong love of God in your son's life, take him along on your own quests of faith. He'll be hooked and forever ruined for the ordinary.

JUST FOR FUN!

Rent or buy the movie *It's a Wonderful Life* and make it a habit to watch it every year. This is a great, entertaining way to bring home the point that heroes don't always go on exciting adventures out in the world. True heroes are heroes of the heart and that makes everyday, ordinary life the greatest adventure of all. Most of the old Jimmy Stewart movies like *Harvey* or *Mr. Smith Goes to Washington* have timeless truths that will nourish the minds of young boys.

Six Ways to Make Faith an Exciting Adventure to Your Son

1. On-the-spot prayers—pray quick short prayers for guidance when you are lost, for calmness when you are frustrated, for wisdom when you need to make a decision. These can be done in the car while you are driving (eyes open), but it is even better to suggest that your son pray for you both.
2. When God answers your prayers, or those of your sons, take a moment to talk about it in a spirit of gratitude and, if possible, pause to give praise.
4. Ask what your son wants you to pray for, write it down somewhere to let him know his request is significant to you, and also buy him a prayer journal and ask him to pray for some of your needs too.
5. Write a scripture on a note card. Tuck it in his backpack, tape it to the door (so he finds it on his way to school), or on the bathroom mirror. Encourage him to pick a favorite scripture and write it down to give to someone in the family who needs some comfort or cheer. Most Bibles have a place where there are suggested verses for specific situations. For example, "When you are sad, read. . ." Or "When you feel afraid, read. . ." Show your son how to use this tool and/or a Bible concordance.
5. Give him a morning blessing. As he heads off to school, you might routinely speak the blessing of Numbers to him: "May the Lord bless you and keep you, may His face radiate with joy because of you" (TLB). To this day, when I travel to speak, my parents often say, "May the Lord bless and keep you, Darlin'," as their parting words. It's a verbal gift that I always treasure. Or perhaps you can give him a

more simple blessing such as, "Remember we love you and God goes with you today."

6. A nighttime blessing might also become a sweet family tradition. One of the most precious memories that my longtime friend Dean Dykstra has from his childhood is of his father's nightly "tucking in" and prayer. His father would warm his boys' blankets in the dryer on cold nights, then tuck each of them in until they were toasty warm before praying with them at night. The tactile memory of a warm blanket and loving hands helped Dean remember prayer as an especially loving time with his father.

POINTS TO PONDER

As we walk this adventure of faith with our sons, it is extremely important that they know God always hears our prayers, and always answers them even when we don't understand the answer. Bad theology can do so much damage to hearts, both young and old. Here are three truths that we need to know to keep our faith from crashing when we are hit by one of life's earthquakes. And we will all be hit at some time. We cannot protect our children from pain; we can only teach them the lessons of resiliency and dependence on God.

1. God never promised a sparrow would not fall to the ground. He only promised to be *with* the sparrow when it fell. There are no guarantees in our life with God except the guarantee of his presence. And he will never, ever leave our side—not even for a split second.

2. A wonderful old quote to teach your child is, "Sometimes God calms the storm. Sometimes he

lets it rage and calms, instead, the child" (source unknown). Both are miracles.

3. I tell my kids (and myself!), "Sometimes the sun shines from the outside in. Sometimes, however, it rains outside, and then the sun has to shine from the inside out." My good friend and local radio personality Ethel Sexton always closes her segments with a wise reminder, delivered in her marvelous Texas twang: "Make your ooowwwnnn Sunshine!" Good advice.

Fresh Manna from This Morning

I have to share something that happened this morning with you, my reader friend—something I feel the Lord would have me insert in this chapter at this point in time because it's so relevant to what I've been writing thus far.

I have a dear author and speaker friend, Lindsey O'Connor, who writes and speaks mostly about motherhood. Her most well-known title is *If Mama Ain't Happy, Ain't Nobody Happy.* Some of you may have read Lindsey's books or heard her speak. Less than two months ago, Lindsey and I spent a week alone together writing on book deadlines in Colorado. (Yes, this book was my project at the time!) Lindsey was eight months pregnant at age forty-one, and this would be her fifth baby. Lindsey lost her mother when she was in her early thirties and has no sisters, so I decided to fly from my home in Texas to visit her in Colorado Springs again when her baby came. Two days before I boarded the plane, I got the news that Lindsey had delivered a perfect baby girl; however, her dazed and devastated husband had to tell me that Lindsey had complications from a ruptured uterus that caused heavy internal bleeding. She was, and still is, in a coma.

I flew to see my beautiful, lively, passionate friend lying helpless in an ICU, tubes everywhere, a ventilator helping her breathe. I won't even try to describe the emotions, as there are no words. Then I went to see her wonderful family: the soft, sweet newborn angel, Caroline; optimistic, compassionate Allison, who is nine; energetic, enthusiastic Collin, who is twelve; precious, nurturing, fifteen-year-old Claire; outgoing, loving nineteen-year-old Jacquelyn; and her godly, brave, grief-stricken husband, Tim.

Today, at this writing, it has been three weeks since Lindsey delivered her baby, and her book. Both were labors of incredible love. She completed her manuscript (ironically on the importance of a mother's spiritual life) just days before she went into labor and had sent me an email: "Rejoice with me! It's done!"

We do not as of yet know whether or not God is going to heal Lindsey or take her home. You can only imagine the trauma surrounding all who love her.

Last week Lindsey's daughter Allison turned ten, and I wanted to send her a special birthday present. In fact, I took my son Gabe along for the ride to a country boutique for this purchase. He didn't want to come in the "girl store" so I let him wait in the car, but I shared with him what happened when I went inside, and today was able to share "the rest of the story" with him by phone, bolstering his faith when he is questioning why so much sadness has happened lately in and around our family. My sharing with Gabe is a perfect example of what I mean by including your children in the adventure of faith—even when, *especially* when, circumstances don't make sense. We cannot shield our children from suffering. But we can teach them about the very God who will never let go of their hands, no matter what comes their way.

Here is the rest of the story, as I was able to share with Gabe: When I stopped in the boutique, I told the woman about Lindsey and that I wanted to purchase something special for Allie, her daughter, who had turned ten the week before. The woman, a sensitive believer, said, "I've got chill bumps from my toes to my head. Becky, I hope you don't think I'm nuts but I know exactly what God wants for her to have."

She then picked out a tiny charm bracelet with three charms: one that said "big sis," a heart that said "mother and daughter," and a letter "A" with a guardian angel peeking out of it. "Now tell Allie this represents her angel that is watching over her all of the time."

I wrote Lindsey's best friend, Kathy Groom, to ask for the O'Connor's address and told her of the bracelet. She wrote back, "Becky, I am in tears. Did you know it was Lindsey's tradition to give each of her girls a charm bracelet on their tenth birthday?"

I had *no idea* about this. But I was able to share this story with Gabe and we both knew that this was no ordinary coincidence. We had seen God at work in a child's life. What a faith booster for both of us!

A Boy After God's Own Heart

2 Samuel 11

Moms, this biblical lesson assumes that your son is old enough and knows the basics of sex and the meaning of adultery. The Bible can be very blunt, but always relevant. Kids are growing up fast in this world, and if your son is old enough to understand this story, it contains valuable lessons that may very well prepare him for temptations of adolescence. Read through the David and Bathsheba story first, and feel free to skip some of it to make it age-appropriate.

This tale of David's sin is a tragic one, but shows how easily a hero can fall—as can we all, especially if we take our eyes off the adventure God has for us. How did David end up in a place like this? He went from being God's chosen king—mighty in prayer, victorious in war—to a self-centered criminal who committed adultery and murder, without feeling any guilt or pity!

Perhaps the key to David's downfall was that he had pulled back from adventure, from God's exciting plan for his life, and let himself become tired and bored and at loose ends.

1. Read verse 11:1 again. What did the kings usually do in the spring of the year? What did David do? Who did David send to do the job he was supposed to do himself?

2. There's an old quote that says, "An idle mind is the devil's workshop." What do you think that means? Do you think an idle mind might have been why our great hero David got so offtrack with his life?

Just Do It!

Though our Bible reading stops at a sad place today, remember this isn't the end of David's story. One day, not too far in the future, David will be called "A man after God's own heart." Sin hurts not only ourselves but so many other people. When we realize the bad things that we've done, we can be thankful that we can go to God for forgiveness and healing.

But the best path in life is always to avoid becoming so weak that we are tempted to sin. What are some ways you can keep your life with God as an adventure so that sin isn't nearly as tempting? Write them in a notebook and reread them often to help keep you focused on the goal ahead for your life.

A Verse in Your Pocket

Here's a wonderful verse from Psalm 32, a psalm of David's after he confessed his sin and found forgiveness. The words *sin, iniquity*, and *transgressions* are all fancy words for doing something wrong. *Acknowledged* means that David agreed with God that he had done something wrong that hurt God's heart and the hearts of others.

Then I acknowledged my sin to you and did not cover up my iniquity. I said, "I will confess my transgressions to the Lord"—and you forgave the guilt of my sin.

PSALM 32:5

Chapter 8

Fluent Guy Talk

Understanding Your Son's
Communication Patterns

Because of a recent speaking trip away from home, I hadn't seen my son Gabe in three days and couldn't wait to see him Friday night after his football game. I thought he played a terrific game, but apparently he fumbled the ball at an important point and was in no mood for small talk—or even a hug or pat—from his mother. Though I was saddened by this, I knew enough to let him sulk. By the next morning I hoped his mood would have brightened, and we could get to that much-awaited mother-son chitchat I'd envisioned.

However, by the following Saturday morning, not only had the sun not risen in Gabe's head, dark clouds were storming in his eyes. I had to take him to school for the follow-up film of the game, where coaches would dissect every play. Gabe dreaded this so much that he could barely mumble "See ya later" to me as he exited the car and walked, as if to a guillotine, toward the high school gym.

I have to admit, my feelings were somewhat hurt, but having just read a book called *Real Boys* as research for this very project, I was comforted to remember that boys have moods too. However, there is a huge difference between the way boys get out of bad moods, and the way our daughters overcome their low emotional days. This time, I determined to apply what I had learned and simply remain quiet, saying few words except a couple of phrases of empathy.

By the time I picked up Gabe from the filming, his mood had sharply turned a corner. I was all ears, and he was all talk, and we had not only a great afternoon together, but a fantastic weekend as well.

In times past, I might have handled Gabe quite differently, disciplining him for being rude and distant. I could have also played mothering martyr. I can take on that role quite well; I've watched lots of Italian movies. "I've been gone for three days thinking of nothing but seeing my youngest son—and *this* is how you reward your mother? You mumble? You turn a cold shoulder? What sort of child have I raised who would treat the mother who birthed him like this? And you weighed ten pounds and two ounces too; don't forget *that*. I have stretch marks down to my kneecaps from carrying you, and you can't take a moment to hug me now?"

So what new insight allowed me to wait patiently for Gabe's return to the world of normal, friendly communication instead of grounding him to his room in frustration and hurt? I'm happy to share what I have gleaned and offer it to you as a potential detonator for future blowups between you and your son.

The Timed-Silence Syndrome

According to Dr. William Pollack, author and researcher for the book *Real Boys,*

> The most challenging time for communication, the time when mothers and sons are most likely to disconnect (although in their hearts they may long to connect even more closely), is when a boy is hurting. I have found that when boys suffer a blow to their self-esteem or otherwise feel sad or disappointed, they often follow a pattern that I call the "timed-silence syndrome."

Pollack goes on to explain that a boy's first reaction to pain is to retreat and be alone to nurse his hurt. (Remember how men tend to retreat to their "cave" from the famous Mars and Venus research? Well, our boys have mini-caves, so it seems.) "If a mother presses him with concerned questions at that point, it only intensifies his sense of shame and causes him to retreat further or more angrily. In many cases, it's only after he has had time to sit with his own pain that he becomes ready to come back and talk about it."

Moms, when he does come around, it can be easy to miss the clues! Pollack continues, "At that point his approach might be so subtle that his mother could easily miss it. And my studies show that if a parent misses that moment, the opportunity to connect about that episode might take a while to come around again."

So what's a mom to do? Try to understand this pattern. When your son walks into the house, obviously upset, you—as a sympathetic woman—may want him to talk about it. When he says, "Leave me alone," you might be tempted to react the way we want men to react when we say, "Leave me alone." A female "Leave me alone" often really means "Come closer, give me a hug and some attention." But when a boy or a man says, "Leave me alone," they amazingly mean they really want us to leave them alone. For a while anyway.

If you can keep from taking this trend personally, when your frustrated, hurting boy comes down the stairs or out of his room and makes a cautious overture of some sort, indicating that he wants to talk, you won't react to the previous rebuff with anger at his rudeness. Just remember that the gruffer your son's "Leave me alone!" is, the deeper the wound is to his ego. It is really a call for you to hang around and be there for him when he's ready to talk later.

POINTS TO PONDER

According to Pollack, "Mothers should feel free to follow what they have always known in their hearts to be the truth—that when he maintains an ongoing connection to his mom, a boy is taking an important, healthy step toward becoming a man." In addition, "A mother is often an expert at coaxing a boy to be more emotionally expressive, feel more confident about himself, and reveal his complete personality with more courage and honesty."[8]

[8]Pollack, *Real Boys*, 112.

Car Talk

Browsing in a large bookstore recently, I picked up a book and laughed out loud at the title: *If Men Could Talk*. Research shows that little girls' verbal skills are generally far superior to boys'. Preschool boys tend to use lots of noises, grunts, and *vrrrooommm* sounds in their vocabulary as they push blocks down with hand-powered Hot Wheels. Little girls, on the other hand, are over in a corner creating intricate dialogues and scenarios between Ken, Barbie, Baby, and their plastic neighbors—and single-handedly doing the voicing for the entire cast.

The two halves of a female brain are used with equal dexterity, because our Creator gifted us with a larger bundle of nerves at the base of our brain. This allows females to talk and think almost simultaneously. We have instant access to both the thinking and speech parts of our minds. In fact, we girls often don't know that we think about something until the moment we begin talking out loud.

Not so with boys. According to authors Bill and Pam Farrell, the male mind is like a waffle. Men and boys think about a subject (one square in the waffle at a time) before speaking, then they speak on that single topic for a while. To change topics involves a disconnecting and re-engaging process. (Imagine unplugging the thinking part of the brain, then plugging into the talking part of the brain, one activity at a time.) Too many subjects coming at males all at once can literally exhaust their minds with all that connecting and disconnecting and reconnecting again.

Women, however, are more like spaghetti, where numerous topics flow in and out of our minds—and mouths—effortlessly. In fact, the more subjects we cover, the more we typically enjoy the conversation.

So what's the best way for you, a female, to converse with your son, who is obviously a male? Pick a topic he likes and stick with it for a while. Plumb the depths of the latest video game he loves, or the new kid at school, or his favorite football team, or whatever he wants to talk about at the moment. Boys also tend to open up to conversation more easily when you do something active with them, like hiking or biking or raking leaves or working on some project side by side. I call this "by the way" conversation. Greg Johnson discovered that his boys would open up and talk to him most as they sat in the outdoor hot tub on wintry Colorado evenings. (Feel free to use this, with my generous permission, as a great excuse to invest in a Jacuzzi.) Other places that I've discovered that both Gabe and his buddies will open up to me is in the car, shooting hoops, playing a game of Ping-Pong, or even going for a walk. These can spark "active talk"—conversation centered around an activity. This takes the pressure off them of having to communicate in a vacuum of silence and gives their brains time to process information between saying what is on their minds.

I've also found that getting absorbed in my own interesting project and generally ignoring my kids seems to bring out the talker in their souls. No sooner do I get involved in a good book, or write the perfect paragraph, then I look up to find a child at my elbow ready to talk turkey or times-tables or angst-filled teen topics. I know it is frustrating, moms, but we have to take advantage of these precious moments and force ourselves to put down the page-turner, pry our hands off the keyboard, and focus, focus, focus on our kids. For they will never pass this way, on this day, again.

> SHOOTIN' THE BREEZE
>
> Sometime, when your son is in a good mood, talk about the different ways you each like to be shown love the most. According to *The Five Love Languages*, author Gary Chapman says that we tend to prefer one or two of the following expressions of love: (1) verbal praise, (2) gifts, (3) acts of service, (4) touching, or (5) focused attention. Ask your son which way(s) he prefers to be shown affection.

The Mother Tongue

Psychoanalyst Jim Herzog refers to the importance of moms gently pushing a boy to stretch his capacity to talk about feelings as teaching them the "mother tongue." How we do this is important. Try the following:

1. Use "I remember when. . ." stories to describe times in your past when you felt sadness or embarrassment in order for your son to know that these feelings are universal. It takes some of the sting of awfulness away from his own difficult times.
2. Help your son find words to describe his feelings. At the right time, ask, "Are you okay? Are you disappointed or angry about something?"
3. Let him know you understand that there's a double standard in masculinity that asks boys to be both nice, sensitive guys and rough, tough guys. If your son believes you really do understand and empathize with this push and pull on young men in our society, he'll be more open to learning the emotional skills you're probably wanting to impart to him.

4. Talk to your son about the men you love and admire and why you enjoy them. Male-bashing is all around us and your son probably has heard more than he needs or wants to hear about what men do wrong. Our sons need to know the positive things you see and admire about good men.

5. If your son is hurting, there's nothing wrong with asking him if he wants to talk. You may just want to be more subtle about it. For example, rather than saying, "Hey, you are in an awful mood. Want to talk about it?" you might say, "It has been a while since we've had a chance to catch up. Do you want to get some pizza together tonight?"

6. Don't hold back on affection. Research shows the power of mother love and that boys who receive generous, appropriate affection from their moms grow to be emotionally literate, secure men.

JUST FOR FUN!

Here's a great opportunity for some "active talking" with your son. Borrow or buy a book about how to fold and make all sorts of paper airplanes and have fun seeing whose airplane flies the longest or highest. With good illustrations and instructions, plain white paper, and a few paper clips, this is a great side-by-side activity that may also open up some moments for conversation by-the-way.

A Boy After God's Own Heart

Read 2 Samuel 12:1–13

Sometimes all the talking in the world just doesn't convince a guy of anything! We just read about David's sin and, at this point, David doesn't really understand how badly he hurt other people when he chose to do wrong. In fact, he thought he might be able to hide this whole mess from God's eyes.

1. Who did God send to David to get his attention? (12:1)
2. How did that person show David he was wrong?
   One thing about God is that he knows how to get our attention! He knew David wouldn't listen to how what he'd done was wrong, or feel any sympathy for Uriah unless he heard a story about another man who sinned.
3. Why do you think the prophet used the illustration of a pet lamb? Do you think David, as a shepherd boy, might have had a favorite pet sheep?

Just Do It!

One great way to get your point across to anyone who has trouble hearing your point of view is to tell a story that shows how you feel. Pretend that a football player in your school treated a friend of yours named Jason very badly by making fun of him in front of the other kids in the lunchroom. Make up a story to try to help the football player understand how Jason might feel. (Hint: It will help if you somehow use an illustration involving the sport of football in your story.)

A Verse in Your Pocket

In the New Testament, Jesus knew that the best way to "preach" to the crowds and keep them interested was simply to tell stories that illustrated a heavenly truth. Sometimes the Bible calls these stories about truths "parables." Everyone loves a good story! (And very few people like to be preached at!)

Jesus spoke all these things to the crowd in parables; he did not say anything to them without using a parable.

MATTHEW 13:34

Chapter 9

Support Your Local Single Mom

(Any of Us Could Be Her Someday)

I hurried through my morning devotions centered in the book of Malachi. Certain passages soothed me and answered some nagging questions I had been wrestling with for a long time. I especially found comfort from parts of chapters three and four, and the sweet promises they offered of healing and renewal. By the time I finished, however, I glanced at the clock and realized I was running late.

Though my friends gave me perfect directions to the airport for my flight from Colorado to a speaking engagement in Tennessee, I all too typically turned left when I should have turned right and consequently missed my flight. My life has been so chaotic lately that a missed flight—even though it would make me late to the church that evening—was, as my west Texas-born mother would say, "No hill for a stepper." A few years before, a missed flight would have sent me spiraling into a frantic frenzy. Now, in light of real tragedies that had been unfolding this year on a nonstop level, a missed flight was way down at the bottom of my panic list.

In hindsight, I have always seen God take most of my honest mistakes (or idiotic miscalculations) and gently weave them into his plan. Why worry when he is in charge of our days? There was an old TV show we used to watch (I believe it was *The A Team*) that spawned a catch phrase in our family: "I love it when a plan comes together." Well, especially when we travel, I believe God and his angels have a blast. My parents recently said that when they head out on a trip of any sort, they have a feeling that Jesus climbs in the backseat with them, eager as they are for the adventures and connections ahead of them. With us on the move, he can mix us believers up and place us next to anyone he chooses.

This particular afternoon, God allowed me to sit next to a handsome young man who smiled generously at me when I sat down. *Now, that's a sweet kid*, this mother heart of mine thought right away. Then I promptly dropped my cell phone under his seat, and his slipped under my seat. Within the next few seconds we had accidentally criss-crossed our seat belts, laughing as we untangled them. His overstuffed backpack just barely fit under the seat, and my own purse was bulging at the seams. We kept apologizing for any inconvenience our disorganization might be causing each other.

At one point, I looked up at this young man, all of eighteen years old, and said, "Honey, if you weren't young and black and I weren't middle-aged and white, I think we'd be twins."

He laughed and from that moment on, though I didn't know his name, we were buddies.

"Where are you heading?" I asked him.

"I'm going to Tennessee to start my first day of college!" he answered with enthusiasm.

"Congratulations!" I encouraged. "You must be so excited."

"Oh, yes ma'am, I am," he said. "I can hardly believe I've made it. I spent so much of the last year filling out scholarships, just hoping and praying that my dream of getting a good education would come true."

"Who inspired you with that dream?" I asked.

"My grandmother," he said, "the sweetest woman in the world. She raised me and about twenty other kids."

"She must be *some* woman."

"Oh, she *is*. I'm already homesick for her. When I was a little boy, about six years old, she rescued me."

"Oh?" I asked.

"Yeah," his voice grew soft. "My mom was mentally ill and to get money for her addictions, she would send me out to sell drugs before she would give me any food. I didn't know what I was doing. I was just a hungry little kid doing what I was told. And then, some of the men she had around also abused me. . . ."

"I am so sorry. This must have been awful."

"It was, it was. But my grandmother figured out a way to get me out of that situation, and eventually got full custody of me. I was such a mess that the school teachers wanted to put me in a special class, but my grandmother wouldn't hear of it. She said, 'All that boy needs is a whole lot of prayer and a whole lot of love.' And she was right. She loved and prayed me into the person I am today."

I wanted to stand up and cheer for this single older woman who had taken upon herself the daunting task of raising not only this bright boy but many others on a meager income, armed with an abundance of love and prayer.

Eventually my new friend nodded off to sleep and while he slept, I prayed for him and wrote out not only my prayer but a special scripture. When our plane landed, I handed him what I had written, told him how proud I was to meet him, and how I was excited for his new adventure ahead. Tears welled up in his eyes as he talked more openly of his love for Jesus. I also shared some of my own struggles and how Christ had been there for me too. Before we left the plane, we stood in the aisle and embraced each other, both declaring that we felt a connection so deep that it was if we had known each other forever.

"You know what?" I asked as I stepped back from him, wiping away a tear. "I don't even know your name, son."

"That's right," he said. "I forgot to tell you. It's Malachi."

I've never met a person named Malachi in my whole life. What were the odds that I'd bond with a young man who's name reflected the book of scripture that had so ministered to my aching heart that morning?

As soon as I had a chance, I reread the passages that had touched my heart. In light of my conversation with the young man, Malachi, the scriptures took on an even deeper meaning.

"Then those who feared the Lord talked with each other, and the Lord listened and heard. A scroll of remembrance was written in his presence concerning those who feared the Lord and honored his name" (Malachi 3:16).

I thought of how the Lord might have heard our airplane conversation about him, and even written down our names!

"They will be mine," says the Lord Almighty, "in the day when I make up my treasured possession. I will spare them, just as in compassion a man spares his son who serves him" (Malachi 3:17).

I thought of how the Lord spared this child by sending in a grandmother to save him and raise him to become the Lord's own special treasure.

"But for you who revere my name, the sun of righteousness will rise with healing in its wings. And you will go out and leap like calves released from the stall" (Malachi 4:2).

The day before I took this flight, I had been walking near a pasture and noticed a farmer letting a young calf out into the field. I found it hilarious when the calf began mooing its heart out, following me as I walked until I finally stopped, went up to the fence, and petted it. Then off it went, leaping in the tall grass, satisfied. It was as if it just wanted a little motherly affection before it went out to play.

So, it was with Malachi. His grandmother gave him all the motherly attention he needed as a little boy, and now she was able to send him off toward a new adventure, to play in the big wide world. Malachi looked so happy, I swear if he'd have been a calf, he would have been leaping down the ramp.

Never underestimate the ability of a single mother (or grandmother), with the Heavenly Father close by her side, to raise a godly, compassionate, confident son.

It Could Be Any One of Us

Like so many Americans, I watched poignant segment after segment about moms who lost husbands and children who lost fathers in the anniversary of the 9-11 attack. Women like Lisa Beamer are leaning on their Heavenly Father and other good friends in the community to raise her children in a home of love, peace, and joy—in spite of the suffering and loss. I know dozens of divorced women struggling to raise their sons and daughters alone because their husbands abandoned not only them, but their children as well. I also have a dear friend struggling to parent her children as her husband serves a prison sentence. Their Friday night ritual includes a long drive to the prison to visit Daddy behind bars. Others are divorced with their kids' dads still involved, and some are married to men who have no clue how to be good fathers or stepfathers. So many women are shouldering at least part of the duties of traditional fathers.

JUST FOR FUN!

Have a regular date night, or encourage a mentor to have one, once a week with your son. It can be anything from going out for ice cream, playing a sport, having a Friday night pizza and video night, to going to a skate park (if you dare!). Make it just one night a week so your son can look forward to the sheer fun of it and good companionship too.

In my book, *Real Magnolias*, I wrote about my friend Tina, who was left to raise two boys alone (ages five and seven) when her husband died of a brain tumor in his early thirties. During our interview of her thriving survival, one of the few times Tina choked up was when she talked about finding one of her sons by the side of the church, crying during the annual Easter egg hunt. "All the other boys have daddies," he cried. "I miss mine!"

If you are a single mother, grandmother, or caregiver raising your sons alone, may I offer you an enormous figurative hug. I applaud you, and I feel enormous compassion and respect for the load you carry—a double load—and often you carry it feeling like a second-class Christian because you don't have a husband and a "traditional family" situation.

To those reading this book who have husbands who are good fathers, pause for a moment and thank the Lord for the help you have in rearing your children, even if your husbands are not perfect. Then try to imagine what it would be like to have to go through this road of parenting alone. Could you do it? Do you ever wonder if you could make it, if called upon to be mother and father to your children?

Of course, you could do it. The story that opened this chapter is proof of that fact, as are thousands of young boys raised in single-parent homes who grow to be wonderful young men. But it would be difficult, and you'd need all the help you can get. If you are a single mom, your job is not only to raise your children, but to reach out and ask for help. If you are in a traditional family, perhaps the Lord will use this chapter to encourage you to take a single mom and her kids under your family's wings, at least occasionally.

> ## SHOOTIN' THE BREEZE
>
> Ask your son if there is any new skill or skills he'd like to learn. Talk about a variety of ways he could get some help in learning new tasks, games or skills beyond paying for expensive private lessons. (Perhaps he could trade mowing someone's lawn for guitar lessons, for example.)

Lone Ranger Mom Seeks Tontos

Trying to parent solo and be everything to your child without asking for help will eventually leave you exhausted with little left to give. Here are a few suggestions that might keep you from burning out.

1. Cry uncle! Though you may have to ask several times, swallow your pride, and be persistently proactive, seeking out good, godly, trustworthy men who will mentor your son or sons, and take the roll of an uncle.

2. If you look for several men to help out, no one man has to feel overburdened as a father substitute, but rather, your son can grow up surrounded by several adopted "uncles" throughout his young life. If your boy plays a sport, you might tell the coach about your situation and ask him to give your son some extra nurturing on the sidelines, telling him the sorts of things a dad might say. A good-hearted coach who can say, "Good job, son!" will go a long way in meeting a young guy's need for a man's approval.

3. Youth directors, uncles, grandfathers, and scout leaders are often willing to take special interest in your son. And even if your child has a terrific father, every boy can benefit from having access to men

who are experts in areas of special interest to your son. For example, if your child is interested in space exploration, try to hook him up with someone who works at NASA. If he shows an aptitude for the guitar, find an encouraging male musician who is willing to give your son lessons. For every interest your child has, pray for God to bring along a male mentor to encourage your son to grow and learn.

4. Don't underestimate the role of other single moms and their kids, or single-parenting groups that can often be found at large churches. All of the women interviewed who had lost husbands on 9-11 had found the most comfort from getting together with other single mothers in their same situation.

5. It's nice to find other single moms who will "stretch" you. For example, if you are a homemaker, indoor type, purpose to seek out a single mom who loves camping or canoeing or something a little outside your comfort zone and experience. This will provide your children with a wide variety of activities and experiences—things a father in the home might have done.

6. Youth camps of all sorts are terrific places for your child to experience living with and around good male role models. Often they can bond with their CIT (counselor-in-training) who will oversee their camp cabin, as well as youth directors or coaches.

7. Big Brothers, YMCA, Boys and Girls Clubs, Boy Scouts, AWANAS programs, or other after-school programs can provide you with some time off at a reasonable (or free) cost, while also exposing your son to others in leadership.

Though there is the myth that boys' heroes are distant figures like sports stars or action heroes, research shows that, in reality, most boys find heroes closer to home. Here are some quotes from boys about their heroes in the absence of a father in the home. Note that if at all possible, boys will most often look to relatives as mentors. Enlist family help!

In Pollack's book *Real Boys*, he quotes who young people say their mentors are:

"My mom is everything to me. She's sacrificed so much so that I can go to good schools. She got me into art, which is what keeps me going, and what I hope will be my profession someday. . . . All the opportunities I have now are because of her."

"Who is my hero? My brother—definitely my brother. He is older so I always looked up to him. . . . We're best friends. . . . He has really been my role model."

"When my father wasn't around, my grandfather was the one who taught me how to pitch—he was my father figure and I look up to him, like, even to this day. He is definitely my mentor. . . . He's just like a great guy."

"I adore my grandparents—they mean the world to me. I spend as much time as I can with them. . . . [My grandmother] would always read books to me when I was really young—all types of novels. My grandmother is an amazing cook. Anytime I go down there, they feed me like six or seven times a day."[9]

---

[9]Pollack, *Real Boys*, 175–76.

A Boy After God's Own Heart

Read 2 Samuel 4:1; 9:1–13

When the news came to the royal palace in Gibeon that both King Saul and Prince Jonathan had been killed by the Philistines in a battle, panic set in. The servants were terrified, knowing how ruthless the Philistines were and that anyone connected to Saul or Jonathan would be killed. Jonathan, David's best friend, had a small five-year-old son with the long and complicated name of Mephibosheth. So let's just call him "Mephi" for short. The woman who cared for Mephi, like a modern-day nanny, grabbed him on the run, tripped, and in the fall broke both of Mephi's ankles, leaving him unable to walk well ever again. This young son of a prince grew up in simple poverty, his identity kept hidden. In those days, people did not treat crippled people well. To make things even worse, Mephi's name meant "seething dishonor." Life was hard on this kid.

Years later when David, now king of Israel, asked for Jonathan's son to be brought to the palace, Mephi must have been terrified that he would be killed.

But David tells him, "Don't be afraid," and then offers him love and acceptance, something he may have never received in his whole life.

1. What exactly did David do for Mephi to show his care? (vv. 7–13)
2. "What did Mephi say to David's offer of kindness at first?" (v. 8) Did Mephi think very highly of himself?

Just Do It!

Is there someone you know who has lost a parent by divorce or by death who needs a friend? What about someone who is handicapped in some way? What could you do to show him love and acceptance?

A Verse in Your Pocket

Memorize the following verse and notice the ways David showed kindness to Mephi.

"Don't be afraid," David said to him, "for I will surely show you kindness for the sake of your father Jonathan. I will restore to you all the land that belonged to your grandfather Saul, and you will always eat at my table."

2 SAMUEL 9:7

Chapter 10

That's All Right, Mama —
Let 'Em Learn Any Way
They Do-ooo

Making Lifelong Learners

I never saw it coming.

Perhaps I should have noticed when Gabe grew his naturally black sideburns long and began to mumble his words in a soft southern voice. Maybe I should have asked more questions when my son asked me what a ghetto was and how we could lend a helping hand to angry young men. A big clue might have been when he began expressing gratitude for small favors by saying, "Thank you, thankyouverymuch." Or the way he went from calling me "mom" to "mama."

Ladies and gentlemen, Elvis isn't dead. He lives upstairs in my house, first bedroom to the left.

I'm not sure when Gabe became an Elvis fan, but he is obviously not alone in his fascination. In fact, this week I spoke at a Baptist church and a woman dressed in conservative church lady attire (navy print dress, white lace collar) said, "You do know you are speaking on a very special day today, don't you?" When I looked puzzled, she said, "This is the day Elvis made his radio debut!" Elvis attracts all kinds.

I've always loved that rich Elvis voice, and "Love Me Tender" still makes my knees weak, but I am most grateful to Elvis, not for his musical legacy, but for helping my son to read.

Let me explain.

All of my children love books, like their mom, and from the moment they brought home their first grade reader booklets, they took to the written word with enthusiasm. All of them, that is, except Gabe. Though Gabe loves math and science by nature, he declared he hated reading from the moment he had to memorize the alphabet song, and almost a decade later he continued to make the same statement. These deadpan, immovable declarations of being a nonreader have nearly sent me into fits of apoplexy at times.

"You can't *possibly* hate reading, Gabe! I'm your mother and I *love* books. I *write* books."

"Well, I don't like to read. Accept it, Mom. Not everyone is like you."

"But books are full of adventure, of stories! You never have to be bored in this life if you have a good book by your side."

"I'd rather eat bugs than read a book."

"You are just being negative!"

"I like being negative. As long as I don't have to read anything about negativity."

I'd try to buy him all sorts of books on fascinating subjects to try to tempt him to read, but after a while we began sounding like some mom/son version of a Dr. Seuss book.

Me: "Try it, try it, you will see! Here's a splendid mystery!"

Gabe: "I do not like those mysteries. Not a curious bone in me."

Me: "Would you like one with a joke? Would you read it with a Coke?"

Gabe: "I do not like books, can't you see? Give it up, already.

I would not like one with a joke.

I would not read one with a Coke. . . ."

And on the story went.

Then one spring, Elvis entered our lives. Girls loved Elvis and guys thought he was cool. Then my dark-eyed, handsome son discovered he was a near Elvis look-alike. That did it.

Suddenly, Gabe had an avid interest—and the only way to discover more about his singing idol was to r-e-a-d about him. And read Gabe did. Websites, books, and magazines. Books for kids, books for adults, books for teens! (There I go with the Dr. Seuss bit again. Somebody *stop me.*)

Not only did Gabe begin to read, his interest in Elvis broadened to an interest in the whole era of the '50s and early '60s. One thing led to another, and the next thing I knew Gabe was interested in history, biography, music, art, and even geography (especially in where Tupelo, Mississippi, and Memphis, Tennessee, were located).

It took a while, but I finally discovered Gabe's weak spot and was able to lure him into reading as a means to an end.

The moral of this story?

Your son may act like nothin' but a hound dog when it comes to certain subjects at school. But that's all right, Mama. If you feel lonesome tonight in your efforts to help your son enjoy certain school subjects, the first suggestion I have is to find out what rocks your sons socks and support that interest. Then tie it in to his learning in every creative way you can.

One for the money, two for the show, three to get ready ... now, go, moms, go! Let's rock, uh-uh, everybody let's rock...

So Much World to Explore!

How does a mom help her son become a lifelong learner? Besides targeting and supporting your son's natural interests, in large portion it is by making what they learn in the classroom practical and *fun* at home and in everyday life.

There's not room or space to cover all of the subjects and great activities out there, but here are a few idea starters to get your brain ticking. . . .

Social Studies and Geography
Where in the World Are We?

I bought two huge laminated maps to display in my office at home: one of the world and one of the United States. (You can purchase them at an office supply or teacher store.) I refer to them all the time since I travel to speaking engagements, but I never dreamed how much my kids would also enjoy them. Put a different color sticker or push pin in places anyone in your family has traveled to. Be sure to have a globe on hand somewhere too—even a cheap blowup globe ball will work (and double as a beach ball in a pinch).

As you learn about various countries and cities—by watching movies, videos, reading historical, biographical, or geographical library books—have your son put a sticker on the places he most wants to visit someday. You might even plan a special trip upon his graduation from high school—somewhere he has researched and is longing to go. You could start collecting your pocket change in a big jar for this, with the words "Our Dream Trip" written across the front. It will heighten the anticipation and make the trip seems even more special. (And yes, Gabe's planning a big senior trip to Graceland. Need you ask?)

Let your son collect travel folders of various states, cities, and countries that he visits or wants to learn about. You can find these through travel agencies or by entering a city or country in the key word section of your Internet search engine.

Here are a few great places for kids to learn geography on the Internet:

- *www.nationalgeographic.com*
- *www.orbigo.com* (interactive map games)
- *www.edu4kids.com* (practice remembering state facts)

No Longer Directionally Challenged

One of my favorite memories was traveling to a family reunion with my daughter, Rachel, when she was ten. Just us girls were in the front, and her little brother was in the backseat. For this special occasion we even rented a little red sports car at a bargain price for the weekend. I purposely put Rachel in charge of the map and she loved it. I had only recently realized the freedom I felt when I learned to read maps—forced to do so when I had to land in new cities and drive rental cars around. I wanted Rachel to experience the self-confidence of knowing she could find her way around the country to anywhere she wanted to go— with nothing but a little know-how and a paper map.

I like to think that because of that fun trip, where I dubbed her "The Navigator," Rachel has never been as intimidated by maps or directions as I was for so many years. In three months, Gabe will be driving and, like his big sister, will be able to find his way around anywhere— as long as he has a map. A compass on the car dashboard is a marvelous tool and will help your child realize that north is not always the direction he is looking at with his geography book in his lap. Line him up with "true north" every so often as you are driving, walking, or observing the stars.

When I was a teacher, I taught my students the four directions by singing a song I made up. First I pointed them toward north in our classroom (you can do the same in your son's bedroom, even labeling the walls). Then we'd sing, "North is just in front of your nose, south is behind your head and your toes. Raise your hand toward the morning light, that is east—what a beautiful sight. Now raise your left hand, it's pointing west—these are the directions that I like best!"

Cooking around the World!

One fun way to explore the world without leaving home is to find cookbooks at garage sales or used book-

SHOOTIN' THE BREEZE

Ask your son where he wants to go on your family vacation this year and let him be a part of the planning. Look at a map and allow him to trace the shortest route to take. Ask him to do some Internet or library searching and make a list of things he wants to see and do on the trip.

stores with recipes from around the world. Have an Italian night or a Mexican fiesta! It's also fun to visit ethnic restaurants, beyond Chinese and Mexican food, if your budget allows it. Try Thai noodles or Ethiopian sponge bread at unusual ethnic restaurants found in most large cities. Guys love to eat and with that temptation in front of them, they will soon love to cook.

You could also invite over foreign students and have them describe their culture. Or, if your son has friends from another cultural, ethnic, or religious tradition, invite them over to your home for dinner or a pizza night and start a conversation about how holiday traditions are celebrated in each of your homes. One mother I know does this with her child's tennis team around Christmas and this gives her family an opportunity to share about their Advent tradition and ultimately what Christ means to them. It turns into a relaxed opportunity for friendship and evangelism.

History

Probably the best way to get interested in history is to start with a great biography or historical movie. Once your son finds himself interested in one person or character (real

or fictional), he will become interested in the surroundings and time period almost by the way. Elvis and the era of the '50s and '60s are Gabe's interests right now. Zeke loved movies about castles and knights in shining armor, and so the Middle Ages fascinated him. Zach loved the humor of Roald Dahl and British comedies. (I've lost count of how many times he played the video of *Monty Python and the Holy Grail.*) Zach has a fascination with all things English, including the history and the books of C. S. Lewis.

Lois Lowry has a gift for creating memorable young heroes and heroines set in historical periods. In her book *Number the Stars*, set in Denmark in World War II, a child hides her Jewish best friend and embarks on a heroic mission to save her life. The Orphan Train series is another favorite, set in the Old West, when orphans from cities were sent to pioneering families by train.

Grace Products has some of the best "visual biographies" I have ever seen for kids in this eight- to twelve-year-old age group. Reg Grant, a friend of humanity and a true Renaissance man, plays the old librarian who takes kids back in time to view a historical event in this series of professional, high-quality videos. All of my children, various ages, boys and girls, thoroughly enjoyed these videos.[10]

A great read for moms is a book called *Moms Who Rocked the World* by Lindsey O'Conner. Lindsey combines her writing skills to create a fiction, time-travel, and factual history novel that brings women in history, like Susannah Wesley, alive to modern mothers.

One of the best ways to bring history alive is to read a book (or listen to a tape or CD) about a certain period

___
[10]You can order the videos by calling 1-800-527-4014.

of time, then travel to the actual setting of the event or visit a museum. My friend and editor Bucky Rosenbaum lives in historic Nashville, and every year there is a reenactment of a scene from the Civil War at the actual site of the battle. As I recall, the drama begins in a cemetery and the actors pop up from behind the tombstone under which the person they are portraying was buried. (Talk about holding a kid's attention!)

Fort Worth, Texas, has a Log Cabin Village where kids can try their hand at spinning wool or dipping candles— and many cities have this sort of hands-on-history in their community. Williamsburg, Virginia, is a favorite vacation destination for families who want to see Colonial history come alive.

I once hosted an Old Fashioned Day in our country neighborhood that will always be remembered as one of the most fun days our children ever enjoyed. In one part of the backyard my builder husband, Scott, dressed like Ol' Abe, and erected a log-cabin playhouse. My sister-in-law set up her quilting frame in the front yard and the neighbor across the street brought her horse to give the children rides. There was bread making in the house, candle making on the front porch, and guitar playing by the barn. We gave the children twenty minutes in each location, then rang a bell and they moved on. We ended the day with a potluck picnic and hand-cranked homemade ice cream. Everyone was tired, but the weather was perfect, and a feeling of contentment was pervasive. As we watched the sun set and the children having a ball, the grown-ups—used to running off to work with briefcases and waving at one another—got a taste of old-time front-porch sittin' and visiting.

Now that was a history lesson—for all of us.

Practical Math
Kitchen Table Calculating

My boys learned to cook as a method of self-preservation, since I burned dinner so often that the smoke alarm became our dinner bell. When you teach your young man to cook, using measuring cups and spoons, take a moment to look in the front or back of a good cookbook (the old red and white Betty Crocker is great) to the Table of Equivalent Measurements. It will tell you, for example, that there are 16 tablespoons in 1 cup; 3 teaspoons in 1 tablespoon. Have your son become familiar with these as he learns to cook, and then sit down with him one day with a couple of recipes in hand. Using what he knows about math and fractions, ask him to double the recipe. Then triple it. And so forth. Ask him relevant questions like, "If you are going to have thirty guys over for an end-of-the-year party, how many pizzas will you need if each pizza serves five guys? How many liters of soda will we need if each boy drinks about sixteen ounces?" Pizzas and pies give great opportunities to divide and conquer the concept of fractions.

Bedroom Geometry

Let's say your son asks to redecorate his room. Use this for an opportunity to help him understand some applicable geometry. (As an aside, does every boy ask his mother at some point if he can paint his room black? What's up with that? I never gave in to this request, but I've decided it must be some sort of guy thing.) Can he figure out how many square feet he needs to cover the walls? Give him the price per gallon of paint and tell him how many square feet the paint will cover. Let him figure out how many gallons he'd need and how much it would cost to repaint his room.

What about letting him think about new carpet (even if you can't buy it, it's fun to dream)? How many square yards would he need to cover his room? Let him look at carpet prices and figure out the approximate total cost of new carpet for his bedroom.

On a smaller scale, small models of buildings, castles, and houses are fun projects and teach your son to use rulers and measurements on a small scale. These can be found at hobby stores.

Shopping Math

Gallon milk cartons, pints of cottage cheese, quarts of orange juice, and liters of cola provide visual measurements for your son to observe. As you are shopping for groceries, ask him things like how many quarts of orange juice could fit in this one gallon of milk?

Store coupons and clothing sales are great ways to help your son learn percentages. Can you teach him how to figure out what 30 percent off a $50 pair of Levi's would be? I highly recommend Ellie Kay's books on saving money. Ellie is a hilarious mother of five, and the best bargain-finder this side of the Mason Dixon. For moms, read *Shop, Save and Share*. For kids, *Money Doesn't Grow on Trees*. See *www.elliekay.com* and tell her Becky sent you!

Word to the Wise

If your son is struggling with math and you cannot help him, ask around and find someone who happens to be great at the subject to help him right away. Often a fellow student is the best help, because they know exactly what the teacher is teaching, and the method he's using to calculate in class. Don't drag your feet on this; get him back on track as soon as possible.

In fact, my daughter is struggling with a college trigonometry class right now. I wouldn't know a function from a firefly, but I did know enough to tell her to call her big brother, Zeke (the math brain of the family), before she gets behind! Gabe seems to be following in Zeke's footsteps and, like many boys, is finding that math is his best subject.

If your son is naturally good at math, but struggling with reading and writing, there's an excellent way to use his analytical skills as a springboard to the "wordy" subjects: Play Scrabble.

Surprisingly, those who play Scrabble in professional tournaments tend to be men who are excellent at math, logic, and spatial skills, who used learning vocabulary as a tool in order to play the word game well. I've found this true with Gabe, who generally does not like word games. However, the math and logic involved in Scrabble are so fascinating to him that he's learning words in order to win the game.

Science

Vegetable or flower gardens are great fun and not only teach your son the joy of planting and watching something grow, but he can also observe science in his own backyard! You can often find large seed packets designed specifically for children's gardens with giant sunflowers, directions for how to grow green-bean tepees, and a nice variety of easy-to-grow edibles.

You can even plant sweet potatoes (with eyes) in a cup of water and produce a nice green vine across the kitchen or bedroom windowsill. And presoaked beans in a paper cup are still as fun to watch sprout as they were when you were in school.

Sprouts are like instant plants and are much fun to grow because you can eat them in just a few days. Buy sprout seeds at a health food store along with the jars to rinse them in. Or you can use Ziploc bags with holes poked in the bottom (with a toothpick) to drain the water as you rinse the seeds each day. My kids liked sprout, peanut butter, and banana sandwiches.

Buy or borrow some pocket guides to birds and plants. Go hiking in nature and see what you can identify together. Make a nature journal of your discoveries.

Fill a net bag (like the kind that fruit comes in) with bits of cloth, dried grass, yarn, dryer lint, or cotton. Hang the bag outside and watch the birds pull out what they need to build their nests.

After visiting a planetarium or reading a book on the constellations, go outside on warm, clear nights to look at the stars and find the Big Dipper, the Little Dipper, and so on.

A friend of mine who lost her husband makes a regular habit of going outside, blanket spread on the ground, to look at the stars. She and her boys talk about their daddy together during these times and how he might be looking down at them from heaven. When I visited her, the boys started begging to look at the stars as soon as the sun went down!

Create a Science Lab!

A tinkering spot (which you can call a "mad scientist lab") can do wonders to keep kids busy in inventive play. You can section off a spot with good lighting, a table or bench, a small Peg-Board for arranging tools, and some shelves and bins to store supplies. You can even add a small couch, old chairs, or a rug. This gives them a spot to ponder as they think up projects.

What are some things you can put in their lab?

- Age-appropriate tools—pliers, files, small Phillips and flat-head screwdrivers
- Broken appliances like toasters or blow dryers with the cords cut off (avoid items with vacuum tubes— TVs especially—anything with chemicals and clocks with tightly wound mainsprings)
- Household castoffs such as an old computer keyboard or a broken light switch
- Scraps of wood, nails, screws, and wood glue
- String, lightweight rope, and pulleys (A fun afternoon project might be to invent a way to pull snacks from the kitchen to the lab!)
- Large rubber bands
- Wire and wire cutters (again, make sure your child is old enough to handle these)
- Plastic plumbing pipes and fittings
- Marbles and Ping-Pong balls
- Magnifying glass, magnets, prisms, or other basic scientific equipment

What will your boys do in this lab? Some will spend hours taking apart old appliances to see how they work, while others might fiddle with sticks and rubber bands to make a shooting contraption or make an artistic arrangement with wood and coins or wire.

Thanks to the authors of *Keep Your Kids Busy—The Lazy Way* for most of the above ideas. This is a wonderful resource book for keeping your kids entertained creatively and easily.

"Spending time with your children can be an invaluable way to bring out each child's natural curiosity. One of my favorite places to spend time with my children is in nature—the places God has created. Let's say you and your child go for a walk in the woods and find a beaver pond where she begins to discover how beavers live. Then you go to the library and read about beavers. From there you go to a science museum and see an exhibit on beavers. Suddenly your child has developed an interest in something she might never have thought about."

—Donna Erickson, host of *Donna's Day*

"Kids are a lot smarter than you think. They don't know what they can't do."

—Nicole, age fourteen

Countertop Chemistry

Here's an amazing little trick for your budding chemists:

Fountain of Foam

You'll need
- a small bowl
- a measuring cup
- tap water
- one package unflavored gelatin
- a teaspoon (for stirring and measuring)
- 3 drinking glasses
- 3 teaspoons baking soda
- 3 teaspoons alum (found in the spice department of grocery stores, used with making pickles)
- a pie plate

1. In a small bowl, mix the package of gelatin with ¼ cup hot water to make a gelatin solution. Little fingers will enjoy poking this gooey mess.
2. Stir in the baking soda and 2 teaspoons of the gelatin solution in the ½ glass of water.
3. In the second -½ glass of water, mix in the alum.
4. Place an empty glass in the center of a pie plate (to catch the foam overflow).
5. With a wild look in your eye, announce that you will create some foam. Simultaneously pour the two solutions into the empty glass. (For effect, you can mutter like a mad magician as you pour.)
6. Whoa!!! Look at all the foam!
7. Good thing you have some leftover gelatin solution. Your kids will want to see that wild mountain of foam erupt again and again.[11]

Raisin Bobbing

Put three raisins in a clear cup of fizzy 7-Up (or other clear soft drink) and observe them bob up and down. Ask your son why the raisins float up and then back down, and up again. (Answer: The bubbles form around the crevices of the raisins and these air bubbles rise to the top of the cup. When the raisins reach the top of the cup, the air bubbles burst and the raisins sink until the process starts all over again.)

Mad Scientist "Gloop"

This is a fun "ooze" to make, touch, and play with! Boys love this.

---

[11]Barbara Nielsen and Patrick Wallace, *Keep Your Kids Busy—the Lazy Way* (New York: Alpha Books, 1999).

- 8 oz. bottle household glue
- big bowl
- 1 cup water
- poster paint in several colors
- 1 cup warm water
- 1¼–2 tsp. borax powder
- small bowl

1. Squeeze the entire bottle of glue into the big bowl. Fill the empty glue bottle with the water and add it to the glue. Stir well.
2. Add several drops of paint.
3. Mix the warm water and borax powder in the small bowl and stir. Don't worry if you can't get all of the clumps to disappear.
4. Stirring constantly, carefully pour the borax mixture into the glue mixture.
5. Stir with your hands until the goop forms globs and oozes easily from your hands.

Tip: If any goop gets on your clothes, wash it out immediately with soap and water.

Science Book Picks

The Magic School Bus Series by Joanna Cole (Scholastic Trade)

With its funny, wacky teacher, Mrs. Frizzle, and adventuresome Magic School bus, this series is highly recommended for engaging kids in all sorts of scientific exploration—from studying space, to under the sea, under the ground, or inside caves! Available at most public libraries and children's bookstores. I used these books as often as possible when teaching children about the planet. The humor and interesting little pictures and charts make this series enjoyable learning at any age.

The Glad Scientist Series by Karol Ladd (Holman Bible)
Four books filled with exciting experiments that teach about God through the science lessons. Topics include *Meet the Creator*, *Visit Outer Space*, *Explore the Human Body*, and *All about the Weather*. You can purchase these as a set and save money on Karol's website at *www.karol-ladd*.com. If you are teaching your kids at home, consider sharing the costs of the set, and passing around the blessing within your home-schooling group.

> ### JUST FOR FUN!
>
> My sister, Rachel, mother of my ten-year-old genius nephew, Trevor, says, "I *love* flip calendars with quotes or other information—whether humorous or serious." You can pick up several at 75 percent off in January at most bookstores. She recently bought one that gives word origins (where words or phrases came from, like "let the cat out of the bag" or "sarcophagus"). Rachel finds them very interesting and her kids get a kick out of them as well. "In other times when I needed a boost, I have a lot of "positive thinking" flip calendars, and I often tape some of the better ones to the family bulletin board. Sometimes I slip one into my child's backpack or lunchbox or tape it to his bedroom door. And the large, picture calendars can be a fun resource too for surrounding you and your son with pictures, humor, or shared interests."

A Word about Overload

Before your child ends up doing so many extracurricular activities that he needs to carry a day planner (and you spend your life in the car), ask yourselves, *If my son adds this activity to his life. . .*

1. will he have ample time for homework?
2. will it affect family or church-related activities?
3. will it interfere with the private time he needs to rest and relax at home, or with time with friends?

Make a list of priorities. Have your son list all the things he'd like to do, if he had unlimited time and energy. Then get realistic and choose one or two per semester. Often he can try a new activity in the next school semester or sports season.

If you find that your son is sleepy, his grades are slipping, or he is just generally cranky, reconsider his activities. We know how easily we moms pile too much into our lives; our children are capable of doing exactly the same thing—only they may not realize they need to back off and slow down.

Teacher-Parent Relations

Encourage your son, in any subject, to talk to the teacher as soon as he starts getting that "foggy, I'm lost" kind of feeling. Teachers are often most receptive to students after class or after school. If the teacher seems extremely busy, your son can leave a note on her desk politely asking when and how he might be able to get some help for a subject he's struggling with. If this brings no response, you will need to call and kindly inform the teacher that your son is in need of some extra help and ask how you can best get it for him.

Study Smarter, Not Harder

If your son is struggling with a subject and you cannot help him, ask around and find someone who happens to be great at the subject to help him right away. As I previously noted, often fellow students are the best help, because they know exactly what the teacher is teaching. Don't drag your feet on this; get him help as soon as possible.

Assure your son that studying in small amounts of time over a period of days, with rest in between, is the best way to retain material. Five minutes of studying a day for five days is always better than cramming an hour the day before the test—even though you've actually spent less overall time studying. A little bit every day adds up.

Learn the tricks of the memory trade. If you have ever participated in Walk Thru the Bible classes or listened to someone on an infomercial teach you how to memorize long lists of facts, they use the same teaching method. They associate and create word pictures in their minds, because our minds think in pictures.

For example, let's say your son needs to know that the mockingbird is the state bird of Texas, the pecan tree is the state tree, and the bluebonnet is the state flower. Have him imagine the shape of Texas in his mind, then encourage him to make up the most outrageous, moving picture he can with the other three items on top of the imaginary shape of Texas. For example, he might see the mockingbird flying around with a granny's blue bonnet tied around its head. The bird could then land on a tree branch that is oddly shaped like pecan pie.

Remember to make your picture wild and crazy—your brain will recall it easier. Also, if you can put "action" in the picture, you will have a better chance of keeping the items in your head. Have your son practice the above technique by playing the game where you put several odd items on a table from a grocery bag or box. Ask him to try to remember all the items on the table. Then put them away where he can't see them and ask him to write down everything on the table he remembers. Practice makes perfect and this little memory device has saved many students at test time.

Another time-tested way to learn something well is to teach it. Tell your son to pretend he is teaching a room full of stuffed animals or action figures how to multiply fractions or write a good paragraph. If he can actually talk out loud and pretend he is teaching something, his retention of that information will double. You know the old saying, we teach what we most need to learn. Sometimes we have to pretend to teach in order to learn.

Hassle-Free Homework

A good rule of thumb is that your son can come in after school, rest, have a snack, read, or play outside and unwind for a bit. But there can be no TV or video games until homework is done.

Encourage your son to make good use of free time to study and do homework at school. The more he gets done there, the more time he has to play at home!

If you find that homework assignments are eating up all of your son's extra free time and your family time, talk to the teacher about possibly cutting back on the amount of homework she is sending home. Your son needs time to unwind from the long day of sitting in a desk to go run and play!

In addition, we have found having a small open hanging file holder on the kitchen counter works great for sorting and signing school papers. Every member of the family has a file where he can put any papers that need to be seen or signed by Mom or Dad, and Mom or Dad can put them in the child's file when they have signed and read the report.

A Boy After God's Own Heart

After David and Bathsheba's first son died, the Lord blessed them with a second son named Solomon. Today we are going to look ahead in King David's life, and fast-forward to a look at his son Solomon.

Read 1 Kings 3:3–28

1. What did Solomon ask God for?
2. What did God give him?
3. How did Solomon choose which mother the baby belonged to?

In school you will learn many facts, and they are very important. Facts usually add up to more knowledge. However, wisdom is even better than knowledge. Wisdom is the ability to know the best thing to do in any given situation, with the help of God.

Near the end of his life King Solomon wrote the book of Ecclesiastes. In this book, Solomon calls himself the Teacher and says, "Because the Teacher was wise, he taught the people everything he knew. He collected proverbs and classified them. Indeed, the Teacher taught the plain truth, and he did so in an interesting way" (NLT).

Don't you wish all your teachers taught in an interesting way?

But Solomon also adds, "Of many books there is no end, and much study wearies the body." I'm sure you've felt this way after a long week of homework, eh? What Solomon is saying here is that knowledge and school learning is great, but it never ends; there is always something new to learn and sometimes that gets exhausting and overwhelming. Solomon tended to overdo *everything* in his life trying to find excitement—even studying too much, if you can imagine that!

Solomon concluded at the end of his life that the best thing we can do is to respect God and obey his commands. This is where we find wisdom, and it is deeper and more lasting than knowledge. It is where the real, lasting excitement is found in life.

If you can get knowledge and learning from books, school, and studies, how do you get wisdom?

Just Do It!

Solomon also wrote a whole book of the Bible called Proverbs, a book full of nothing but wise sayings. Here is where you can find the secrets of wisdom! Open your Bible to Proverbs 10 and read a few of the proverbs of Solomon. Which one do you like the best? On a piece of paper, write down the proverb and illustrate it.

A Verse in Your Pocket

In the book of Proverbs, Solomon talks about his father, David, and the advice that he gave to the young prince. It was great advice then, and it is great advice for us today.

My father told me, "Take my words to heart. Learn to be wise. Don't turn your back on wisdom, for she will protect you. Love her, and she will guard you. Getting wisdom is the most important thing you can do!"

PROVERBS 4:4–7 NLT

Chapter 11

What Matters Most

Eternal Perspective for Moms and Sons

It always amazes me how the world as we know it can change in an instant. Most life-altering events occur within a ten-minute span of time, but the magnitude of those minutes can make them seem an eternity.

Ten days ago, at the writing of this chapter, I experienced just such a moment. I was driving to speak at a church in Tennessee on a Saturday morning when my cell phone rang.

"Becky," my husband said, his voice heavy with pain. "Call home. We've lost Joshua Gantt. He drowned last night at his dock after jumping in and getting tangled in fishing line. Gabe and I are here for the family, but Melissa needs her Becky."

"Oh, God," I cried, tears filling my eyes. "He's only nineteen. He's Michael and Melissa's only son and Sarah's only brother. . . ." I could not see to drive and pulled into a hospital parking lot to catch my breath and weep.

For those who have read my other books, my dear friend and neighbor, Melissa Gantt, will be a familiar name. We were "Ethel and Lucy" friends on a wild, adventurous trip to California in *Milk and Cookies for Grown Up Kids*. She was my chick-flick gal pal from *Coffee Cup Friendship*, the one who picked me up in Josh's Mustang convertible to see the movie *Hope Floats*. (Melissa had cleverly grounded Josh from the use of his own vehicle, in part, so that we middle-aged moms could borrow it and feel young and cool again.) And in *Real Magnolias*, she was the big-hearted woman who gave her kidney to a neighbor's dying child.

In the companion book for this series, *Mom's Everything Book for Daughters*, Melissa is the mom who called with the exciting news that her son, Joshua, and my daughter, Rachel, were officially boyfriend and girlfriend. (This story took place several years ago.) Their romance lasted only one sweet summer, but Josh gave my daughter her first real kiss. I'll never forget Josh dropping by one morning, not long after their breakup, flashing his famous grin that never failed to light up any room he ever entered.

"Come here, Josh," I'd said. "I want to talk to you a sec."

He walked over and leaned against the door frame, his dark hair framing a movie-star face. Tom Cruise had nothing on Josh Gantt. "Yes ma'am?"

"I just want you to know that it's okay with me that you and Rach are just friends again, instead of boyfriend and girlfriend. But I sure hope that one day, when you are both in your twenties and know what you are doing, that you'll come calling for her again, because I'd love to have you for a son-in-law. You are one of the few boys she knows who always make me laugh. It would be fun having you hanging around, and I could be sure that Rachel would have great in-laws."

He grinned and nodded obediently. "Yes, ma'am," he answered. "I'll do it."

My daughter eventually married another equally charming, wonderful guy named Jody, and Josh fell in love with another lovely young woman, but the Gantts and the Freemans remained the closest of family friends. For years, Gabe followed Josh around like a puppy and Josh was always good to him, driving his boat up to our dock and taking Gabe skiing or wake-boarding to my son's great delight. Gabe has always referred to Melissa as his other mom, walking in her kitchen anytime day or night to help himself to a snack—whether she was home or not! Josh's sister, Sarah, and Gabe are known, even at school, for acting "just like a brother and sister." The day before I received the tragic news about Josh, Gabe called me and said, "Mom, all the mothers of football players are gathering at school to have their pictures made wearing our football jerseys."

My heart sank. "Oh, Gabe! Why didn't they tell me this earlier? I'd love to be in that picture, but I have to be here in Tennessee."

"Don't worry," he said. "I'll get Melissa to do it."

"Gabe, you know I want to be in that picture, but I am really grateful at times like this that you have a backup mom. I'll call Melissa and ask her to take my place."

"Naw," said Gabe. "I'll go over and ask her in person. I want to see what they are having for supper."

I laughed out loud. Melissa had often been a lifesaver to me and my children, and in turn I'd been there for her during moments of joy and heartache. Two moms in the trenches, comrades in parenting, friends in the frenzy of life.

But never, ever, could I have anticipated she and I would walk through this deep valley of the shadow.

I glanced at my watch through my tears, jerked back to the current realities. Only ten minutes before I had to be at the church and ready to speak. *Pull it together, Beck,* I said to myself, *one step at a time. You can fall apart later.* Then I prayed aloud, "Oh, Lord, get me through this. . . ."

I drove to the church, explained what had occurred to the event planners, both of whom comforted me, then went to the phones, working to find me an earlier flight home. When I walked up to the platform, I found my legs were buckling, so I asked for a stool on which to sit. Then I opened up one of my books, and read aloud from a classic Melissa and Becky story. After the reading, I shared about the tragedy that had just happened. Tossing the planned talk, I spoke instead on the deep, deep love of Christ that nothing can separate us from. Not height or depth or the present or the future or . . . death. I don't really remember what I said for the next forty-five minutes, only that I felt cocooned and carried by a Presence beyond myself.

I do remember, however, glancing over toward my left and to my surprise, noticing that I'd been speaking for twenty minutes with a huge red handbag looped over my shoulder. I couldn't help but laugh and feel enormous love for this audience. They had felt such tenderness for me in this time of heartache, that they'd refrained from pointing or giggling about my delivering an impassioned message with a purse dangling over my shoulder the whole time. "Did you all think I was going to use this as an object lesson?" I queried, chuckling as I walked over to put my shoulder bag down. Then I added, "I guess this is an object lesson: People in shock have no idea what they are doing."

I called upon all the moms who had lost children to come pray with me for Melissa, and pray they did. One precious mom had just lost her eleven-year-old daughter, two months before, in a car accident. She had received huge measures of love from her church family and a deep peace even in her pain. I felt encouraged at seeing moms who had survived such a loss, knowing that Melissa would make it through this somehow. She had a daughter who needed her. She would find the courage and strength to survive and thrive for Sarah.

When I finished speaking, the ladies wanted to do more, anything to help. So hundreds of us held hands around the inside of the church as together we lifted up the Gantt family to God in prayer. I found out later that during this very hour, Josh's father, Michael, had turned to Melissa and said, "For some reason I feel such a peace right now."

As I started to leave, a woman handed me a little bookmark with a picture of a shaggy shih tzu dog on the front and the verse "We walk by faith, not by sight." "Please give this to Melissa," she said. Moments later I must have dropped it out of my notebook, and a woman came running up to me and said, "Becky! You almost forgot this little bookmark." I thanked her, tucked it in my purse, and promptly forgot about it. I could think of only one thing—get on a plane and get home to Melissa.

I finally arrived at Melissa's house in the early evening, where I enveloped my dear, dear friend in my arms as we grieved together. In between what I came to call "grief spasms"—overwhelming hurt and convulsions of weeping—Melissa and I looked at pictures and talked softly of memories we wanted to cement in our minds.

She held up one of the photographs and traced the face of her son with her finger. "This was taken last weekend, his last picture. He had finally learned to ski barefoot and was having the time of his life." Indeed, that pearly white smile, his dark hair flying in the wind, his eyes sparkling with accomplishment, all said to us, "I'm flying and it's the greatest feeling in the world!" Without saying a word, we both knew that Josh was flying with the angels, and it must be the greatest feeling in heaven.

Being in heaven is wonderful for Josh, but today a brokenhearted mom is still here on earth—and the thought of not seeing her boy walk through the door again leaves a gaping wound that nothing else can fill. Melissa curls up on the bed and wails like a lost little girl. She's a classic mothering nurturer to everyone who knows her, but now she's the one who needs caring and comforting. I lie down beside her, spooning into the curve of her legs, holding her as close as I can until this contraction of grief subsides. I feel like a midwife, providing the only thing I can give—the nearness of my presence as my friend labors in emotional agony. "Oh, dear God," I cry softly. "Comfort my friend." It is all I can pray; it is the sole cry of my heart.

Later that night I walk home and unpack my things slowly, and my fingers brush the bookmark. Suddenly I remember a short scene at Melissa's house from moments before, like a fuzzy background suddenly come into focus.

A few minutes after I'd arrived in the Gantts' living room, an adorable shaggy dog had appeared at my feet, putting its paws and head on my knees. "Where did this cute dog come from?" I'd asked, petting its soft head, gazing into its pleading black eyes.

"Josh found it a couple of weeks ago, brought it home, and named it Wonder Mutt. He loved that dog so much."

As I examine the bookmark more closely I realize that the photo on the bookmark, and Josh's dog were not only both shih tzus, but they had almost identical markings.

Morning came and I drove to the funeral home to pray for Michael and Melissa in a nearby parlor as they go through the excruciating process of making arrangements for their son's viewing, funeral, and burial. Josh, an artsy musical soul, had lived his life since high school the way he wanted to live it—working at a local restaurant by day and performing his songs by night, to the strum of his guitar and the delight of the young crowd gathered at the local Cadillac's Grill. He had worried his mom and dad with some of his unconventional choices, but they determined to love and accept this unique child and whatever gifts God had given him. Josh called Melissa at least every two or three days and without fail they always ended their conversations—however tense or controversial—with sincere I love yous. In the last week Josh had called his mom to say, "Well, you've got a college boy now. I just took my entrance exams and signed up for the fall semester." His parents thought they would be spending this week celebrating Josh's decision to further his education. Who would have dreamed they'd be planning his homegoing service instead?

When Michael and Melissa walked into the parlor, having completed the hardest deed any parent can do on behalf of their child, I gave her the bookmark and said, "I think this might be God's gift of comfort from Joshua to you."

Melissa looked at the card then back at me, sat down on the couch, and said, " How strange. . ." Then she read the verse and, tears standing in her eyes, said, "Becky, Josh was struggling with issues of faith a few weeks ago, and I opened my Bible and read him this very verse."

Within an hour of this incident, the entire Gantt clan—from grandparents down to young cousins—were sitting in the front two rows of church. It had been less than forty-eight hours since they lost their beloved son, grandson, brother, cousin, nephew, friend. Through the series of praise songs, Michael and Melissa stood and sang, their fifteen-year-old daughter between them, with their arms around one another and eyes lifted to heaven. At one point, Melissa slipped me the bookmark, which she had already laminated, and asked if I'd tell the church family about it. I did, and spontaneous applause rose to the God of all comfort, who had given us this tangible token of reassurance in the wake of devastating loss. We know God cries with us, even as he rejoices with Josh on the other side—where everlasting life swallows up death.

The funeral on Tuesday was hours long, with Josh's buddy Jeeter singing two of Josh's original songs. This moment was especially poignant for two reasons: Josh and Jeeter were a singing duo, and it was Jeeter who had dived in to pull Josh out of the water, doing CPR on him for thirty minutes until the paramedics arrived and could do no more to save him.

Our young pastor then spoke of the Old Testament patriarch Jacob, and how he wrestled with God until the break of day. Then he described a God who invites young men and women to wrestle with him over their questions about faith, until they find peace and know that God is God, and we are not. When Josh wrestled with questions, angst-filled heartfelt questions in search of spiritual truth, his mother was there, Bible and heart fully open, with answers.

The last time I saw Joshua, he was singing a song for Melissa at Cadillac's. It was their song, a tune called "Simple Man" that spoke of a mother's desire that her son find a simple life of love and joy. I had put my arm around Josh after the performance and told him, "It's nice to know someone who is going to make it to the big time. I can say I knew Joshua Gantt when he was a kid starting out with nothing but a song in his pocket and stars in his eyes."

In Melissa's honor, the music minister sang "Simple Man" at the close of Josh's funeral service. Her son never made it to the stage and bright lights of the big city, but he had lived a simple life in a small town and, from the overflow at the church, it was evident that this boy, forever young, had lived a simple life of love that had touched hundreds.

Why have I taken all this time to share this story with you? Because watching this precious mother lose her only son, so beloved, has given me renewed clarity in what really matters as we mother our boys. Melissa grieves, but she does not grieve anything unsaid. She doesn't grieve over any regrets for what she did or did not do as a mother. She knows she gave Joshua her love, her total acceptance, and her eternal belief that he was someone very special to God. Her grief is pure pain of loss—like a clean cut—that will eventually subside and ease with time, though her life will be forever changed. It is not the jagged, rough, scarred grief of regret for what should have been done, should have been said.

What would you say to your son today if you knew he'd be gone tomorrow? Go say it; don't let the sun go down before you've done it. Then keep saying it, close every telephone conversation with "I love you, son," hug at every parting, and it will become an automatic lifelong habit. Tell him all the things that make you proud of him, and when he asks questions about God, applaud him for asking them. Then go to your Bible with your heart fully open, and give your son the greatest answer of all: God made you, son. He loves you. Your life has a purpose and when your life on earth is over, you will wake up in a paradise with beauty beyond describing, a place of no tears or sorrow. A place where Jesus walks and talks and reigns, where our family will live together forever.

Don't be surprised if he comes often, especially in the teen years when life suddenly presents many more questions than answers. And do not be shocked at anything he says or asks. Though he may balk at times, playing too cool for Sunday school answers to complicated problems, trust me on this: He really only wants to hear you say that Jesus loves him, this you know, over and over and over again.

Five Things a Father Learned from His Son

Joshua's father, Michael, miraculously found the strength and desire to deliver his own son's eulogy. "I will do this to honor my son and who he was," Michael said. Hundreds and hundreds of people of all ages came to the funeral. Joshua touched so many lives in surprising ways.

When Michael realized how many people loved and admired his boy and the way his unique style affected others, he told me, "Becky, I don't think I've ever been more proud of my son than I am right now." It reminded me so much of the story I wrote about earlier in this book when Dr. Phil had talked about the father who had lost his son suddenly to a heart attack on the basketball court. Once his son was gone, the father realized that the things that once irritated him so much were a huge part of the memories he now cherished and admired about his child.

I leave this shortened version of the eulogy with you as a parting gift, with Michael and Melissa's permission.

The Most Important Things I Learned from Joshua by Michael Gantt

1. Accept Others As They Are and Never Judge Them

Josh always accepted others and respected their beliefs. Countless times he would finally tell me, "Dad, that's you—not me!" He did not have a problem with my opinion; it just was not the same as his. I think one of the reasons Joshua never could understand why people did not accept him the way he was, was because he accepted all people for who they were.

2. Be Honest: Don't Lie Even When You Could Get Away with It

When I was Joshua's age, every time I did something I wasn't supposed to do and got away with it, I felt like I somehow got a point! My son left this life with no points and did not even want any.

Even at an early age, I saw that my son had this trait of being completely honest; he messed up a lot, but he would never try to get away with anything. When he was four or five, he came into the house and told Melissa something he should not have done. At that point, I could not resist it any longer and had to ask him, "Son, why did you tell us what you did wrong?"

At that time, Melissa hauled off and hit me and said I just flunked Parenting 101. Joshua just did not comprehend any other way to live life but to be open and honest—even when others would have tried to hide and get away with their mistakes.

3. Be Loyal and Show Compassion to Your Friends

Josh was always concerned about his friends. As a matter of fact, in the last two weeks he set in place some concrete plans to help some of his friends whom he was truly concerned about.

He was always giving his friends advice and guidance on everything. And from talking to many of them about this trait of his, almost everything he told them was both true and helpful.

4. Say "I Love You" and Hug a Lot

Because of all the emotion this point brings up, today I am unable to talk about this one a lot, but the examples and stories are endless. This I can say: My son said, "I love you" and hugged more in his nineteen years than I have in my forty-two years.

Josh always ended his phone calls with "I love you" and always hugged everyone hello.

5. Do Not Always Associate an Action to the Person

One of Joshua's theories was just because someone does something bad or stupid doesn't mean that the person is a bad or stupid person. When the dust settled on one of Joshua's teenage pranks that got him in a heap of trouble, he made me agree with him that this action was dumb, but that he, himself, was not a bad person.

A Bonus Point

Always respect your mother and call or talk to her a lot. Joshua always respected Melissa, and he called her all the time. I would recommend this to everyone.

My Own Afterthoughts

God carried Michael on a cloud of grace as he delivered the above speech. Then Michael took the paper he had read from, rolled it up like a scroll, and walked down to his son's open coffin, tucking the speech beside his son as he said goodbye. Later, after everyone had gone, I saw Michael, who is normally very quiet and reserved, tightly holding his nephew in his arms (a boy who looks so much like his cousin Josh), weeping the tears of a father who would give anything to be holding his son again.

Moms, I know this is painful to read. It is painful for me to write. But if it can help one mother or father accept and love and communicate that love to their "challenge child," it will have been worth it. And to each of us who has been gifted with a little rebel, a challenge, or a prodigal son, know that we are not only here to teach and train them, but they are also here, in surprising ways, to teach us some important things as well.

Write Your Son a Letter Today

What have you learned from your son? Perhaps you could write him a letter telling him five things he has taught you since you birthed him into this world. You may be surprised how precious this gift will be to him. Don't wait or this moment might pass. Put down this book, grab a pen and paper, and write whatever flows from your heart to his.

A Boy After God's Own Heart

Read 1 Samuel 1:17-27

David receives word one day that his best friend, Jonathan, and another man he loved, King Saul, were killed. Even though Saul's mental illness and sin made him murderously jealous of David at times, David must have felt pity for the king and still loved him. Perhaps David remembered the inner torture Saul felt and how David's harp music calmed him. Also, King Saul is the one who gave David a chance as a little boy to fight a giant. At death, we often remember the very best about someone we once loved.

Later in David's life, one of his sons, Absalom, is also killed. Even though Absalom was a rebellious son who was trying to overthrow his father's kingdom, David grieved over his prodigal boy deeply by crying, "O my son Absalom! My son, my son Absalom! If only I had died instead of you—O Absalom, my son, my son!" (2 Samuel 18:33).

On the occasion of Saul's and Jonathan's deaths, David writes what is called a lament—or a funeral song—for his friends and even asks that all of the people of Judah learn it.

1. How does David want to protect Saul's and Jonathan's names from being laughed at, even after they died? (v. 20)
2. What good things does David say about this father and son? (v. 23)
3. What does David say about his feelings for Jonathan? (v. 26)

When we lose someone to death, our hearts hurt, and we long to find some way to express our love, feelings, and pain. In Old Testament times, funerals often lasted for days, with lots of crying and talking until the grief had lessened some. When the families huddled together at this time and poured out their pain together, they found renewed strength to live again.

Did you know that scientists have found that there are toxins (like poisons) in tears of sadness, but there are no toxins in tears of joy? It is as if God meant for us to cry to get those toxins out of our body. In this way, we release our pent-up pain to God, and the Bible says he saves all of our tears in a bottle. Not just any bottle, but a wine-making flask. This is a picture that God takes our sadness and tears and uses them to create something beautiful and good, that someday will bring joy to others in their times of pain.

Just Do It!

If you have lost friends or family members to death, you could write a poem of lament for them and share it with others who loved the same people. Like David, you could write something about how you are protecting their memories, what good things they did, what you loved about them, how you feel about them being gone, and how you long to see them in heaven some day.

A Verse in Your Pocket

I grieve for you, Jonathan my brother; you were very dear to me. Your love for me was wonderful.

2 SAMUEL 1:26

The Answer Is Blowin' in the Wind

It's Worth It All

Yesterday was Sunday and almost all of my children, two with mates of their own now, came over for what was to be one of the most simply beautiful afternoons I've had in months. I sensed a togetherness, a joy, a maturity, in my children as they make the journey from kids to teens to adults.

Zach—the kid who kept us on our toes and our knees, who poked holes in his eyebrows and ears, who tattooed his back—was my only son who was absent yesterday. However, he came over last weekend to help me put some stepping stones down in the yard, and stayed and napped, and ate and hugged. Though a late bloomer, at age twenty-two, Zach is growing up, preparing to enter the Army National Guard.

Zeke, an architectural student at the University of Texas at Arlington, mowed the yard as his wife, Amy, and I wielded hedge clippers and fought back the wild wisteria. Amy will graduate with her art degree in just a few short months.

Allison, Gabe's girlfriend, helped pick up fallen branches as Gabe manned the leaf blower and cleared the porch of debris.

At one point, I walked into the house and glanced at a packet of wildflower seeds on the kitchen table. A friend had sent them to me, tucked inside a card of encouragement, urging me to plant them as a sign of new life.

I have been reading a book called *The Gift of Mourning Glories*, and in it the author describes her worst year—a year when she lost her husband to divorce, her health to bone cancer, and her job with its income. She writes about how she planted a packet of morning glory seeds and how they came to symbolize a lush new growth of life from what once looked like shriveled, dried-up deadness.

Inspired by the thought of doing the same thing, I took the packet outside and found the perfect spot to plant my flowers. Though they were not morning glory seeds, they would work. I set up a little bench, placed a pot on it, and bent over to gently, meaningfully, prayerfully, sprinkle the seeds in the soil from my outstretched palms.

Gabriel, unaware of my little planting ritual, walked over at that point, aiming the leaf blower at me and grinning wildly. He was hoping to get a laugh for messing up my hair, but the only response I could give him was to stare in unbelief at my empty palms. My seeds! My dreams! Where were they now?

Certainly not in the little pot where I had planned them to go, to stay put, and to grow. They were scattered hither and yon. I will only know where the seeds landed when spring comes and the wildflowers bloom.

So it is with raising children. We think they will stay where we want them to stay and grow where we want them to grow, and the next thing you know, the leaf blower of life carries them in all sorts of directions we never planned for them to go.

And we must wait to be surprised. Surprised by where they will go, and what they will do, and when they will blossom.

But blossom they will.

I can testify to that. My kids and I had a great time of laughter after I told them the tragic comedy of how Gabe had blown away my precious seedlings. After a simple supper, my children found places, like a litter of puppies, to chat, play a game, do homework, draw, snack, and generally remind their mom that Sunday afternoons like this are the reason she went through carpooling, raging hormones, worries about their safety, and prayers for their salvation.

Ordinary, fun, love-filled afternoons like yesterday are the golden blips in time that make raising children so worth the effort.

By the way, I went on a walk today and—get this!—discovered that growing in the wild forest area behind my house is a literal *field* of morning glories!

Sometimes surprises come much sooner than expected.

Hang in there, moms. I'm planting, watering, and waiting alongside you.

Acknowledgments

Special appreciation to the kindness, talent, and encouragement of Sandy Vander Zicht. Your words have lifted me up so often. Your vision for your authors to be writers of excellence is only eclipsed by your personal concern for their lives. Thank you. Angela Scheff, you have been a joy to work with, made the editing process almost painless—and your quiet, persistent patience with my scatterbrained self is amazing.

Also to my literary agent and rarest of friends, Greg Johnson, who also wrote part of the companion series for this book along with the talented, insightful John Trent. I can honestly say from observing Greg's tender and enthusiastic love for his boys, Drew and Troy, through the years, that I've never seen a better father—except, perhaps, my own dad.

To my three sons, Zach, Zeke, and Gabe—you are each unique and so loved. Each of you has taught me more about God and life and resiliency than I think I could have ever taught you. Thank you for loving your mom as you do, and for allowing me the pleasure of watching you grow into manhood, becoming more and more not only my sons, but also my friends. To Jody Rhodes, who had the good sense to marry my daughter and has become just like a fourth son in our family, exactly the guy we needed this year to add to the love, comfort, and joy in our midst. And to all boys who have called me their Other Mom through the years—like David, Duarte, Casey, Dallas, and Drew—

friends of my sons who have become friends of mine. I love each of you. You have multiplied the blessings around our kitchen counter and enlarged this mother's heart. (And kept her on her toes and her knees as well!)

Thank you to my assistant Rose Dodson who not only keeps me organized but has been the shoulder of love that I have leaned upon through a difficult year, a buffer zone taking care of details so I could think, focus, and write.

Welcome to Rachel Praise, my daughter who will follow in Rose's shadow as the newest assistant—part of the village it takes to raise her mom. I love you, sweetheart, and though I know you didn't get your ability to organize from me, I am so glad you have it!

To Jesus, the Father of us all, through whom I live and breathe. When I get up in the morning and face the blank screen with nothing to say of importance within myself, he fills me with words, my fingers fly, and, miraculously, I write.

For more information about Becky's books and speaking information or to contact her with a comment, visit her website at www.beckyfreeman.com.

WOMEN OF FAITH℠

Women of Faith partners with various Christian
organizations, including
Campus Crusade for Christ International,
Crossings Book Club, Integrity Music,
International Bible Society, Partnerships, Inc.,
and World Vision
to provide spiritual resources for women.

For more information about Women of Faith
or to register for one of our nationwide conferences,
call 1-800-49-FAITH.

www.womenoffaith.com

Help Your Relationship with Your Daughter Blossom!

Mom's Everything Book for Daughters

Practical Ideas for a Quality Relationship

Becky Freeman

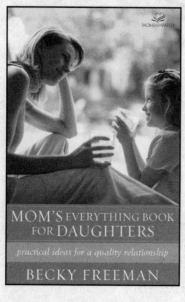

A potpourri of the best, most usable, and most fun advice on how to be a wonderful mother.

How can a woman be the kind of mother her daughter will want to imitate when she grows up and has a little girl of her own? This is an easy-to-digest, information-packed tool to help moms create wonderful, positive memories for their daughters. Written in an engaging, entertaining style, this fun, practical book gives hints on a wide range of subjects.

Softcover: 0-310-24294-0

Pick up a copy at your favorite bookstore!

Create a Bond Between You and Your Sons

Dad's Everything Book for Sons

Practical Ideas for a Quality Relationship

**John Trent, Ph.D.,
and Greg Johnson**

It is crucial for dads to cultivate strong personal relationships with their sons while they are young so that when the turbulent teenage years hit, the bond will be so firm that nothing can separate them. Following the pattern set in Luke 2:52, fathers need to keep a balance by focusing on all four areas of their sons' lives: mental, social, physical, and spiritual.

Dad's Everything Book for Sons is filled with

- Fun ideas on what to talk about (and how to talk about it)
- Special "adventures" dads and sons can do together
- Guy "getaways"
- How to have Bible studies they will both enjoy
- Creative ways to bond—including things he likes to do as well as things Dad likes to do
- Suggestions for volunteering and helping others together
- Prayers to pray for sons

Softcover: 0-310-24293-2
Pick up a copy at your favorite bookstore!

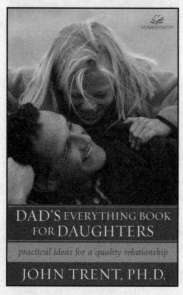

We want to hear from you. Please send your comments about this book to us in care of zreview@zondervan.com. Thank you.

ZONDERVAN™

GRAND RAPIDS, MICHIGAN 49530 USA

WWW.ZONDERVAN.COM